To Robin

R.G.C!

Lots of Love

Willie

Keep Going Clear!

KEEP GOING CLEAR!

A Guide to Better Showjumping

by William Sheret MBE

with David Sheret

Published in September 2016 by Keep Going Clear Limited
www.keepgoingclear.com
willie@keepgoingclear.com

in association with Story Terrace
www.storyterrace.com

© William Sheret MBE & David Sheret 2016
All rights reserved

Special thanks to Kate Smith, Lynne Paterson, Diane Dawson, Duncan Lockerbie & Isla Ewen-Menzies.

Typeset by Lumphanan Press
www.lumphananpress.co.uk

Printed and bound by Bell & Bain Ltd
Thornliebank, Glasgow, G46 7UQ
www.bell-bain.com

Contents

Foreword by Geoff Billington   7

Introduction   9

Biography   11

1. Forever Basics   19

2. Horse Sense   28

3. Tack and Equipment   37

4. Training And Schooling   47

5. Jumping And Competition   61

6. Reflection And Analysis   70

7. Summary   74

Development Charts   83

Testimonials   87

*Dedicated to my late wife Marjory.
As ever, I've kept you a seat.
Love always, Willie.*

Foreword by Geoff Billington

The first time I met Willie Sheret was in 1972. I was a 17-year-old, riding horses for a Manchester nightclub owner called Joe Pullen. Joe was a bubbly character and it was not long before he was parading me around at shows and introducing me to his 'special' Scottish friends. I already had a great bunch of Scottish mates, (guys like Graeme Gillespie, John Brown, Jack Mcgeoch and Andrew Hamilton) from my time competing against them in ponies. However, you can never have enough friends and on that day I added another two. One was Sir Hugh Fraser, owner of Harrods; whose daughter Trish went on to become one of my best patrons. The other was a friendly showjumper called Willie Sheret. Willie rode horses for Sir Hugh with much success and the two horses that stand out in my memory are Arthur of Troy and St Corry (although St Corry was owned by Peter Irvine).

Willie won many big classes on Arthur and I was there the night Willie won the Foxhunter Final at The Horse of the Year Show on St Corry. I cannot remember the atmosphere ever being as electric as it was in Wembley Arena that night. It was like the whole of Scotland had travelled down to support Willie and St Corry. The Scottish are always a celebratory bunch and I would be lying if I said I did not also 'sample the goods' when I was with them. Ah, those were the days, and my passion for all things Scottish continues to this day with my marriage to my beautiful wife Sarah.

Willie was an inspiration to us all and competed into his seventies. When he finally retired he still kept his hand in at the shows and I also remember taking a seven-year-old horse to the Royal Highland Show where the collecting ring steward was none other than Willie. As I came out of the ring he said to me, "That is the best horse you have ever had, son." How right he was because the horse was none other than 'It's Otto' who went on to take me to two Olympic Games.

Whenever I go to any show in Scotland, Willie always comes to find me and invites me to, "Come on back to my caravan, we will take a wee dram!" and I always come out happier than when I went in. I am sure every bit of advice in the book is going to be a treasure and I look forward to reading it and picking up some knowledge along the way.

Here is to the next 40 years of friendship, haha!

Willie Sheret, I salute you!

Best wishes,
Geoff Billington

Introduction

Horses. I firmly believe that there is something inside us that pulls our hearts and souls towards these magnificent animals. It is more than a hobby or a pastime, more than a sport or spectacle. It is a lifelong calling and one that we are blessed to have.

I have been lucky when it comes to horses and showjumping. Over the past 74 years, I have studied, competed in and taught showjumping throughout the UK, Europe and Canada. I have been fortunate enough to have ridden brilliant horses and brought on future superstars. I have managed to win a few big classes and been awarded humbling honours. However, the most fulfilling aspect of my career is, by far, helping riders (of all levels) to develop their talents. To watch a young child jump a cross pole that an hour earlier they could not even look at is still something that gives me enormous pleasure. Watching one of my student's (not to mention their parents') faces beam when they jump off their horse after clearing a height they never thought possible is more satisfying than any of my personal showjumping achievements. Teaching is my passion. I love it.

Therefore, I am delighted to have been given the opportunity to write this book, and also to write it with my son. The process has been extremely enjoyable and as is often the case with projects such as this, I have learned a lot about myself. If there is one recurring message that I would like readers to take from this book it is that everything we do in showjumping must have our love of horses at the core. Without this, we are cheating ourselves and life is too short for that.

So please, read this book with the passion you and your horse deserve. Take what you like, leave what you do not like. What might work for one may not work for another. I am eager to point out that I do not know it all and I have never met anyone who does; although I am sure we have all met a few who think they do! However, what I do know is that combining practise, common sense and honest reflection with tried and tested techniques, and a willingness to learn will make you a better showjumper, of that I have no doubt.

I have put my own development tools at the end of this book so you can set out and evaluate your performance against your goals. And remember, the more you practise, the luckier you become.

I really hope you enjoy the book and 'Keep Going Clear!'

Biography

People often ask me how I became a showjumper and the truth is it was my father that introduced me to horses. He was a coalman in Glasgow and had a number of horse and cart combinations through the years. Before that he was stud groom at Drumtochty Stables in Aberdeenshire and I think that, deep down, he always longed to work with horses full-time. My father was an excellent horseman, not in the sense that he was a great rider or an inspirational coach, but more in his understanding of horses and what made them tick. A lot of his horse sense is conveyed through my words and I hope that he would be proud of the horseman I have become.

In the early days of my showjumping career, I was entirely self-taught. I used my eyes and put in the hours just watching others (a theme you will notice recurring throughout this book). I was ten years old when I first started working with milk horses and I remember clearly the first time I sat on a saddle. It had felt so natural that when I left school at 14 in 1942 I knew I wanted to have a career with horses, so I went to work for Stuart Easton, a scrap merchant in Glasgow, looking after the horses and ponies. The first time I jumped a fence it was a yard sweeping brush. Within a week I was jumping the height of myself; which if you know me, you will understand is a small achievement but an achievement nonetheless.

I started going to shows very soon after, around 1944, I think.

My most vivid early memory of competing was at Drymen Show with a horse called Cutty Sark. As it turned out, years later when I first rode at the Horse of the Year Show, the horse was also called Cutty Sark, and was a foal of the original mare. I understood then that horses' lives often parallel our own and also that we lacked imagination when it came to naming them!

On 6th February 1947 I was called up for National Service and drafted to Germany with the 955 company Royal Army Corps and I became known as 'Driver Sheret'. We were then sent onto Berlin where we camped at the Olympic Stadium. I thought I had seen destruction after the bombings of Clydebank but it was mild compared to Berlin. From the back of the troop carrier all we could see was mile upon mile of rubble. It is a haunting memory to this day.

I was put in charge of the stables for no other reason that I was the only showjumper there. There were over 20 horses and I was also put in charge of 18 German grooms – they even gave me a jeep to ride around in! I went to the yard and met the riding instructor, Herr Von Korus. I could see immediately that he ran a military-style operation despite the grooms being civilians. There was a large arena there too, which the Germans used for tournaments and they even had an indoor school, the like of which I had never seen before. The horses were German and Italian and they were in good condition, but thin. The people in Germany were starving so horse feed was poor; meaning that the horses were rationed and it showed. Things changed a bit after the airlift started though and we saw them improve almost daily. This is a constant reminder to me of how lucky we are to live in the plentiful western world we do now.

It was there that I met a man who changed my life. Otto Klitski was the riding master at Spandau Stables and one day I recall him asking if he could ride my horse. In less than two minutes he showed me, the cocky kid from Partick, that I knew next to nothing. He was a brilliant rider and I later heard, although I have never seen it officially verified, that Otto Klitski came fourth in the 1934 World Championship. He taught me how to ride properly and how to really be as one with your horse, as well as how to bend a horse around your legs both ways and how to turn a horse without reins. He was a genius and I watched his every move. So much of my style comes from Otto.

In October 1947, Otto and I were presented with a horse. It came from the remount station where horses were taken after they were commandeered. It was an unbroken Hanoverian mare called Sally and we knew we had something special when she just walked away with Otto leading her, without a rope being tightened. Sally had a beautiful sparkle in her eye and a really pleasant way about her. She just needed some love and guidance, and to be broken-in.

After a brief break back home to Glasgow, I returned to Berlin. The commanding officer asked me to carry on my duties at the stables. The first person I met was Otto, so we went straight to Sally's box. She was now in pristine condition and Otto had set up a jump at one metre fifty so I cantered her around and faced her up to the fence. I will never forget the feeling as she took off. It was like being on the back of a stag, floating through air with that silence only showjumpers know. She was ready for competition, but it was my other horse Pat that was about to take centre stage.

There were horses coming from all the Allied Forces sectors for the Berlin Championships and I was lucky enough to be selected to compete. During my first round I came to a bascule fence and Pat took off. She was so high I thought she would never land. Her spring was incredible. Everything went well for us that day and I managed to win the event which, if I recall correctly, was called the Allied Forces World Riding Championships. A British Army officer's wife even said to me: "It was like you and the horse were one, you each knew what the other was going to do." That has always stuck in my mind as an ideal, because that was how Otto looked when he rode and jumped, and that's what I have always strived for.

It was a great feeling and one I became thirsty for. The officer in charge of the stables gave me champagne (which I had never seen before, let alone tasted) and I was even reported on in the army magazine. People then started to come out to ride and see the stables. I knew from that moment on that I was going to be a showjumper.

When I was about to demob, the army told me that I had a chance of going to the 1952 Olympics in Helsinki if I remained in service. However, the Berlin airlift had started and I wanted to go home. I think about Helsinki often but I believe that regret is a negative emotion that only saddens the heart. I just smile and content myself with the amusing thought that I would have won if I had gone.

I tried to buy Sally from the army but it did not work out. I came back to Glasgow and bought my first horse, Glencoe, which I schooled and then started to compete and win on. The feeling of winning never lost its appeal and even to this day I like to win – but as you will go on to read, it is not the most important thing!

In my 20s I started a small riding school in a ruined stables with a tarpaulin roof in Bearsden, Glasgow. That was a great experience and I have fond memories of that yard. From there I was asked to take over as manager of the Kilmardinny Riding School before going back to working for myself, again in Bearsden. In those days I did everything that needed doing myself. I became a jack-of-all-trades by necessity, building my own arena and taking cheap, unwanted horses with problems and schooling them into winners.

Another notable point in my life was when I won the Foxhunter at Wembley in 1975 on St Corry. True to my ethos of fixing 'problem' horses, St. Corry had come to my yard from Ireland with the word that she was good but had a 'stop' in her. However, she was not really a problem for me and I soon had her jumping for fun before going on to qualify for the Foxhunter; which is one of the biggest classes in showjumping. She jumped a clear round and I found myself in the jump off against two others, Paul Jones and David Bowen.

I remember every second of the jump off so clearly. The black curtain went back and all the lights were on. I was second to go and my understanding was that the first rider, Paul Jones, had a fence down so my plan was to take it easy and go clear. However, as I started the round steady I heard this voice, which I think belonged to Ted Edgar, shouting "C'mon Willie!" At that point I thought that I better speed up a bit. We jumped clear and I found out I had just pipped Paul who had actually gone clear. I ran back to see how the final rider, David Bowen, was faring and as I came through the curtain he clattered the planks. It was all over. I had won the class I had always wanted to win, achieving the dream I had held since I was a young lad and I was so proud of St Corry. As I rode into the arena to pick up the award and do a lap of honour, the crowd went wild and I took my place on a page of showjumping history. It was, as Geoff said in his foreword, an electric atmosphere. I will treasure the memory forever.

Another high point was when I was awarded an MBE in 1995. By then I had competed in hundreds of competitions with thousands of people watching but I was more nervous that day than any other. It is an honour I cherish. Not just because my son lobbied for it to happen but because it highlighted showjumping. In many ways, I share that award with all showjumpers because without all of us, there is no sport.

As I mentioned, over the years there were horses people could not break or horses that would not jump or were not going well. I would bring them on by positive schooling and that is what I am going to try and leave with you in this book. I have a number of techniques that solve issues with horses but most are common sense. I have been blessed with a good pair of hands and the strong horse sense my father gave me. Normally I can find the key to a horse and this is usually in its mouth.

Good examples of my approach can be seen in the horses I have ridden for various people over the years, and one that stands out is Arthur of Troy, Princess Anne's event horse at one point, I think. Sometimes, like Arthur of Troy, there are horses that are great jumpers but you need to be very careful with them. With Arthur, people even warned me that he could kill me if he took the notion and it is at this point that I will state clearly – horses can be dangerous. Be careful and never, ever take them for granted. You are always learning from the horse as much as they are learning from you. For example, with Arthur of Troy I learned that he was in too much of a hurry so I slowed him down. I would canter him at a walking speed over combination jumps.

As with Arthur of Troy, when you spot something in a horse or indeed a rider that is not quite right, it is a great challenge to fix them. If you can make some tweaks and get them going again, it is really something. For me it is better than winning. I recall a young child whose pony did not know what to do and just would not jump a fence. I set it up to follow another pony and the pony not only jumped the fence, it went right round the course. The girl was so delighted and her face when she cleared the last fence was a picture of joy. That sort of moment is worth a thousand rosettes.

Some people think that ponies and horses just jump without any training or practice and I find that sometimes when I go to teach, people hope I have a magic wand. I have been very lucky with the students that I have worked with and I always emphasise that it takes practice and confidence to jump and to jump well. In the end, it is mostly down to you. A good teacher, in my opinion, allows you to find your best. There are no short cuts and no magic wands.

Showjumping is the sport I love and I like to share my knowledge with everyone that comes along. Hopefully, if I have done my job correctly, they leave with a better attitude and understanding than when they arrived. As a teacher, there is little benefit in making people do things they are not capable of yet because it kills the spirit and can lead to accidents. One of the most common quotes I get from students is: "I never thought I could do that." They just did not believe. So I guess my job is to get them to believe, but safely.

Two of the key components in my philosophy, not just in showjumping but also in life, are modesty and common sense. I always try to pass this on to other people, to explain the mistakes I have made, examined and overcome. If you are modest then you are grounded and if you are grounded then you think sensibly. Add common sense to the mix and all of a sudden you have a foundation that is strong and stable.

I have had an amazing life and I have been very, very lucky to know some lovely, lovely horses. My love of horses fuels my enthusiasm for riding and jumping, which is why I get a lot of pleasure out of teaching.

So there you have it. Now you know a bit more about my showjumping life story. It will hopefully give you a little insight into the approach that has kept me developing and learning over the last 70 years, and which still drives me on every day.

1
Forever Basics

Key Points:

Open Mind – Get & Stay Focused – Bond – Get In Shape

One of the statements that always baffles me is: "Let's get back to basics." It baffles me because I think to myself: Why have you ever left? Basics must always be at the centre of any sport and showjumping is no different. My belief is to begin with the basics and never leave.

Open Mind

First and foremost, if you are going to have basics at the heart of your showjumping then you must keep an open mind. Do not make the mistake that basics are always instilled at the beginning, they are not. Basics are the skeleton of everything we do and we want to instil within us as many good traits as possible at the start of our careers because they will form the framework upon which we develop our style, individuality and success. But basics are simply good habits that collectively improve our performance and consistency. They are something we must constantly be searching for throughout our whole careers. So as a rule, I would say always listen to any advice offered and even if you do not agree with it, store the good and bad advice in your memory and keep them there for basic reference because both are useful. An open mind will help you develop your basic skills that in turn will provide more and more possibilities. Possibilities lead to possible, possible evolves into goals, goals become achievements and achievements equal success. It sounds simple and logical and that is because it is.

A closed mind can be the biggest inhibitor your basics face. No matter how talented you and your horse are, if you do not have the ability to constantly challenge what you are doing then you are essentially restricting your potential to grow as a rider, and indeed as a team. I cannot emphasise this enough. It is easy to default to a closed mind and we have all done it. We will say: "This is how I do it, I do not like the new way, it feels uncomfortable, I do not understand what is being suggested so I will dismiss it." When we do this we become the biggest fence we will ever face. So be conscious of the signs and always lean your mind towards the open position.

Having an open mind is a task in itself and it is always a work in progress so do not underestimate the effort involved. It is also important to say that having an open mind is not to suggest that you copy everything everyone tells you because that is not an open mind, that is an impressionable mind. You have to be able to balance your own confidence and conviction against the need to adapt and utilise considered advice. I have absorbed a huge amount of knowledge by listening to and watching others and I highly recommend that you do the same. I have observed riders and their mannerisms for over 70 years and it constantly fascinates me how much they contribute to their own lack of development.

For example, many times I have watched showjumpers more interested in gossiping to their friends at shows or sitting in their lorries for hours whilst they are waiting to compete. This, to my mind, is wasted time and a clear example of not fully exploiting their opportunities to learn and develop. Of course you need to spend time preparing and you have to enjoy yourself too. Please do not think I am trying to be a killjoy, but you are reading this book because you want to become a better showjumper so it is important that I am honest. Not taking advantage of all the rich, plentiful learning possibilities around you at a show or at any equestrian moment for that matter, is inconsistent with fulfilling your potential. Your peers will have developed a number of basic enhancements through their own schooling such as little hand movements, posture changes, leg positions, course management, horse sense ... the list goes on. These are all there for you to study, free of charge, and you will witness firsthand what works and what does not work. Development and learning opportunities are all around you, so be a sponge, take it all in and feed your open mind.

We are never the finished article and if you think you are then your development is the only thing that is finished. We can always improve and having an open mind means that you are very well positioned to ensure that basics remain forever a companion and ally in your quest to become the best showjumper you can be.

Get And Stay Focused

We will get on to physical fitness later in this chapter, however mental fitness is key and when I say 'mental fitness', what I really mean is focus. You have to ask yourself two key questions at this point:

1) Why do I really want to be a showjumper?
2) What does success look like for me as a showjumper?

When I started out I liked to win and, as I said earlier, I still do. But it is important to put it into context. Winning is a temporary thing and it is not the be-all and end-all. I competed to win (and I would always urge you to do this) but I eventually realised that it was the development of horses that really inspired me, and if I focused on this part then winning often followed.

However, that may not be the driver for you so you have to be honest with yourself and answer the questions above sincerely in order to find the centre of your focus. It is important that you do not confuse winning with glory because glory can often be an empty room once you enter. In the beginning I wanted glory: for everyone to rate me and know my name, but glory has to be handled with care because it is as quick to leave as it is hard to achieve. My advice is to change out glory for satisfaction then let satisfaction become a major part of your focus as a showjumper. If you are satisfied with what you are doing, where you are in your horse's development and most of all, who you are as an individual showjumper, then success, adulation and all the trappings that come with it will be there. You might not become the best in the world but you will be a rounded, happy rider who competes without the inhibitions and insecurities that so many riders carry on their back. You will be focused and content and that kind of rider, in my experience, is difficult to beat.

Bond

Symbiosis. If you look up the definition of this word in the dictionary (and I had to) then it says 'interaction between two different organisms living in close physical association, typically to the advantage of both.'

I can think of no better description for what I am about to talk about but symbiosis is a bit of a mouthful and as the whole point of this book is to make becoming a better showjumper an easier process, I am going to replace it with the word 'bond'.

The bond between a rider and their horse is extremely important. In showjumping, we have two brains working as one and we have to ensure that they are as connected as closely as possible. If you turn a horse to a fence and their mind says no, it does not matter how good a rider you are they will not jump it. End of story. You have to build a strong, two-way foundation of trust, respect and understanding and this starts in the yard. Competitions are never won in the yard but they are certainly lost there. If you do not invest the hours at home then you are putting yourself at a massive disadvantage to the showjumpers that do; and by investing the hours I do not mean jumping over a few fences in a paddock twice a week. What I mean is really putting your heart and soul into building a relationship and a true bond with your partner. Yes, your partner. You cannot win anything without your partner.

So get bonded! Grooming, feeding, flat work, riding out, caring, jumping, even watching them play in the field. There are no short cuts to be found and you should not want to find short cuts anyway. You reap what you sow when it comes to building a bond with your horse, of that I have no doubt.

It is no coincidence that the horses that I have had most success with, I have genuinely loved. We built a bond between us and we went into every competition as a team. Like most relationships, we had our ups and downs. We fell out, we were not talking to each other, then we made up again, then we were on fire and working almost as one. But no matter where we were in our relationship we always had that love and respect for each other. Through good times and bad; it was working on that connection (our bond) that helped us develop as a team.

There are some brutal truths to learn, though, and like the ones we have with our friends and families, relationships with our horses are fickle. We get on with some people and less so with others; it is the same with horses and riders. If you are forcing the issue with your horse, then the chances are it is just not going to work out. This is not to be confused with bringing a young horse on or helping a horse that has had an accident and needs its confidence rebuilding. The route to this kind of bonding is a totally different path and it is a skill in itself. In fact, helping horses develop and recover is an essential part of any horse lovers' duty. If you have not had the chance to do this, then get involved. Horses sometimes need you more than you know.

However, even if your horse is healthy and happy that does not mean it is the best horse for you. If you suspect you and your horse are not progressing, then the question is: how can you tell whether it needs its confidence rebuilding or the two of you are just simply not compatible? Firstly, concentrate on your bond and getting your horse to like you. Spend time with your horse. I understand that people lead busy lives but try to spend as much time as you can with your horse. Get in to the habit of staying five minutes longer than you can spare. When riding, get communicating through your feet and hands and when you are finished riding, step off his back and spend time patting him.

Then, once you have practised the basics as described in this book, try jumping. If you are riding to a jump and your horse feels soft in your hands, then the horse might not jump, or might kid you on and stop. This is because the horse is taking control of you and rushes to the fence, only to stop because the horse has no confidence in you, and he gallops because he is scared. Instead build up your own confidence and the horse's confidence in you by communicating clearly with your horse, working on your bond and not taking them for granted.

Properly evaluating the relationship you have with your horse is also about having the ability to detach your emotions from an important decision, namely: is the relationship we have good enough to realise what we want to achieve? Normally, deep down, you know the answer, so be honest with yourself. As I said, when it comes to competing in showjumping, bond is incredibly important. Make sure that you are aware of its value and ensure that you give it the respect both you and your horse deserve.

Get In Shape

As in most sports these days, fitness is no longer optional. For years, many sportsmen and women have done 'enough' to compete and in showjumping, especially in my day, we were among the worst. However, 'enough' these days is no longer enough.

I have been blessed with being a naturally fit man but I have also worked hard at staying fit. If I was competing today and had the benefit of all the scientific diets and training routines now at our disposal, then you'd better believe that I would have them fully integrated into my focus and routines. I see so many amateur showjumpers, men and women, who are not just unfit, they are very unfit. I do not understand this because it is a key area where you can gain huge competitive advantage. There are four key physical areas that I have in my mind when teaching riders: balance, strength, concentration and endurance. All these attributes are required when you compete.

Let us take a show as an example. You could be at a show for four days. On each of those days you are up at 6am and you will ride six horses in a day, maybe in five classes with two horses in each. You might even ride a few jump offs too, and you finally finish as the clock strikes 10pm. That is a long day. It sounds obvious when we say it like this but for goodness sake, get fit! It will also help you greatly when you fall off; and you will fall off because we all fall off! If you are fit, you will take any impact better and you will most definitely heal quicker.

Be sure to watch your weight too because if you seriously want to compete, then you want to give you and your horse every possible chance. If you are a good few kilos heavier than your competitors, eventually this is going to go against you. We are all built differently and there is only so much you can do, but to put it in context, try jumping over a pole or two on your own, then put on fully loaded rucksack and try again. You start to get the picture. Your weight is, for the most part, under your control and it makes sense that in a sport where the aim is to jump over fences that you are as light as you can possibly be.

However, before you run off and start living on a diet of lettuce leaves and water, please be sensible as you are a sportsperson and being unhealthily thin is as debilitating as being overweight. Your aim should be to be the best athlete you can be and if you work hard and sensibly on your fitness you will see a marked improvement in your overall ability to compete.

Diet is hugely important. I am not a nutritionist by any means but I know that top athletes do not eat fish and chips every day. You have to balance your social life against your ambitions. Go back to your two focus questions and ask yourself if your diet fits in with your answer to both? There is simply too much evidence these days that supports the fact that the better foods you eat the better your body performs. So my advice here is to get some advice. If you would pay for a showjumping coach because you want to become a better showjumper, then you should also be willing to pay for a nutritionist. It is not just about learning tricks and skills whilst riding, it is the whole package, and a good diet will give you a great advantage.

There is not much we can do to combat natural talent, either of a horse or a rider. Talent is a gift and I believe that some people, for whatever reason, are just born able to do things naturally better than others. That being said, you can become more 'talented' by practising harder, of that I am convinced. Aside from natural talent, all the other component parts of showjumping talent we can absolutely improve. We can be fitter, have a better diet, be more prepared, develop greater concentration, work harder, have a greater bond with our horse, and be more open-minded. You can see where I am going with this. So much of becoming a better showjumper comes from working harder than the rest at all the other component parts, and your health, fitness and diet are key here.

So with this in mind, do not see keeping fit as a burden, see it as your 'silver bullet' and a huge competitive advantage. Get a training routine and a good, sensible diet and trust me, you will come on leaps and bounds.

The next chapter looks in more detail at horse sense and the importance of choosing the horse that is right for your stage of development.

2

Horse Sense

Key Points:

Get The Right Horse – Your Advisor – Do Not Just Buy Pretty – Keep An Open Mind – Try Before You Buy – Breeding – Tell-Tale Signs – Reflection – Two Novices Do Not Make Experience – Stay The Course – See The Vision

Loving horses is only one part of it. Horses are magnificent animals in so many ways and they are very much the centre of my life, as I am sure they are yours. This book is focused on helping you become a better showjumper and therefore we need to establish some hard truths. If we do not then I am doing you a disservice. So on this basis, let's get some horse sense etched into our heads.

Some people have asked me if I am a horse whisperer. In a way, this could be said of lots of people who have spent their lives around horses. My father was definitely one. But horse whispering is nothing more than understanding. It comes with practice and experience. Close, respectful observation and thoughtful actions will almost always build a good relationship with a horse.

Unlike with a car, you do not get an ignition key with a horse, and every horse and rider relationship is different. Think of all the little mannerisms and quirks that you are aware of in your own horse already, and the hours you have spent getting to know each other. It takes time and practice and most of all it takes a foundation of good, basic horse sense.

Get The Right Horse

A classic failing in showjumping is when people buy their horse with their hearts, or worst of all, their ego. What does this mean? It means that they buy the horse with emotional and not practical thought. In order to be successful you have to buy a horse that will fit your focus, current ability and personality.

Let us start with focus. You will read this word a lot throughout this book and I make no apologies for it as focus is a key component in developing your ability as a showjumper. So when it comes to choosing a horse, ask yourself this: what is my short-term focus, my mid-term focus and also my long-term focus?

If you are a novice, then your key short-term focus has to be to find a horse that can help you develop safely and with enjoyment. If you choose a horse that is too advanced, then both you and the horse could become frustrated. On the same basis, if you choose a horse that has no real showjumping ability then the chances are you will end up disillusioned.

My advice here is to go to a few shows and watch the classes that you are planning to compete in. Take full stock of what is going on and do not be afraid to invest time too. If you are a novice, then it makes sense to have a knowledgeable person that you trust to advise you on the purchase. Sit down with them and map out a few different shows in different areas to visit. Do not just go to the nearest show either. Be prepared to look at a large number of horses if necessary. Then I would suggest that you get a few key wants and needs set out. Write them down and you will be amazed how helpful they will become.

Your Advisor

This has to be someone with no vested interest in the sale, financially. It should also be someone that is not trying to make you purchase the horse they would like to ride. Your adviser must be interested in investing their time into you and they also have to be open to listening to your point of view. Just because you lack experience does not mean you lack intelligence. You are the one that will have to live with the decision and you certainly know more about you than anyone else. This is a hugely important appointment. Make sure that you do it based on fact, track record, third party endorsement and a little bit of 'gut feel'. Emotion is fine and after all it was probably your heart that got you into showjumping in the first place. Your heart deserves to be heard but it has its place and that place is not at the forefront of important decisions.

Do Not Just Buy Pretty

We all love a good-looking horse but good looks alone only guarantee one thing: that you will have a good-looking horse. Keep at the front of your mind why you are there and what you are trying to achieve. You need a horse that can help you in your quest to become a better showjumper. No more, no less.

Keep An Open Mind

You have two eyes, two ears and one mouth. Use them in that order. You are not trying to sell anything here. Indeed, you are the one with the cash so remember, the most powerful person in this transaction is you. Have your list of key wants and needs set out, and from there, just look and listen. Take notes and get your adviser to ask the questions. That way you can concentrate on observing. Keep your mind well and truly open and keep your heart hidden away. Dealers are professional salesmen. Their job is to make you desire their horse. Your job is to get the best horse you can for the money you have. It is all part of the game and winning in showjumping is not just rosettes and cups. Be smart. Be patient. Be open-minded and again, do not be emotionally led.

Try Before You Buy
It is important to watch the horse go under someone else too as this gives you some perspective and allows you to watch how it travels, collects and generally how sound it is. However, if you buy a horse without riding it then you are asking for trouble. Remember the importance I placed earlier on bond? You have to feel for yourself how the horse goes. Feel is so important in showjumping and it is essential that you ride the horse – and not just for five minutes. Ride the horse for a good half hour at least on your first visit. Start with a gentle walk round the school a few times. Then take the horse into a trot, again for a few circuits. Break into a light canter, change legs at the corners a few times (as we will discuss later) do a few diagonals and then maybe hop over a few ground poles. But most importantly; and you may think this is silly, make sure you can start and stop the horse. It sounds like a given but I cannot emphasise enough how important the basic ability to control your horse is, especially for a novice rider and how often it is neglected.

Once you are comfortable then pop it over a few fences and make sure you put the fences eventually at the height you are planning to compete at. Again, it sounds obvious but I have seen it many times before when a rider buys a horse because they loved it at first sight, gets it home and then finds out it cannot jump for toffee! Make sure your horse is fit for purpose and ideally, but not essentially, that it has a little scope to improve. You always want to try and protect your investment as much as possible and you have to think of the future as well as the here and now. In other words, when you have improved your own ability and changed your own goals, will you be able to sell your horse to someone who can benefit from the time you have invested and also make a profit? There is nothing wrong with having this thought in your mind, however, much like emotion it should contribute to the decision but never have the casting vote.

Breeding

Nowadays in showjumping a significant focus is placed upon breeding and ideally you are looking for a horse that has come from a good sire and a good mare. It makes sense. Getting this part right comes from doing your homework so make sure that you understand the bloodline of the horse you are about to buy. There are never any guarantees but if the horse has a good bloodline then you mitigate a bit of risk. However, breeding is not as important at novice rider level as having a good, sound, experienced horse that can help the rider develop. Be conscious of breeding, yes, but do not see it as essential. Some people love to tell you which sire their horse is by as they lead it back into the box after being eliminated in the first round. Do not fall into the brand snobbery trap.

Tell-Tale Signs

When buying a horse for a novice rider, there are a few tell-tale signs I look for. If I was your adviser I would want to see a horse that has an 'intelligent eye' in its head. What I mean here is that the horse catches your eye when you approach and they are interested in you and want to know you. This says a hell of a lot about a horse. I would also want to see a horse that is balanced, that is to say that the horse will strike off on the correct leg when breaking into canter. I am always looking for a horse that is keen to please too. One that will go to the fence looking at what he is doing with his ears pricked forward and who wants to do the job.

On jumping, I want to see a horse tucked up well in front and throwing his hind legs out behind, without weighted boots. The horse should also have good conformation. I would want to see the horse stand still and then I would walk round it, carefully, to look at it from all sides. The horse should have good posture with strong quarters and a good slope to its shoulders. If the horse is fit it should have a strong neck. If you put your hand across the neck it should be firm and well defined. I would also look at your proportions to the horse's size. There is no point getting a horse that does not fit you. Make sure the horse is as customised to you as possible. I would also be cautious about buying a horse that is standing back on their pasterns or has a slight U-shape to their neck. This shows signs of possible weakness and is, for the most part, inconsistent with a good jumper. Generally, though, it is about common sense. Take your time, have a list of checks, stick to them and trust your adviser.

Reflection

Do not buy the horse on the first day that you see it. If you like the horse and it has ticked the boxes, you are likely to want to buy it right away. That is normal but there are a number of reasons why you should not. Firstly, it is a major purchase and there is nothing wrong with taking time to consider such a purchase. Big decisions like this should not be made in the moment. They should be reflected on and you and your adviser need to sit down and evaluate all the horses you have seen. At this point I would be inclined to shortlist them down to two and then go and see them again, visiting the least favourite second. The reason for this is that you again have the opportunity to go and make your decision whilst not in the moment. You might think that this is overkill and hard work but I would say that if you think that way then you really have to question how much you want to succeed.

So, reflect on the purchase. And please, please get the horse vetted. This is a must to insure the horse at any rate, but it is equally important to have the horse vetted for the 'what will happen' as well as the 'what could happen'. A horse is an investment. Treat that investment with the respect it deserves.

Two Novices Do Not Make Experience

It can be difficult to advise on a set profile for a horse that would suit a novice rider because no horse is ever the same. There are a few guidelines that I tend to default to. Going back to the advice at the beginning of the chapter, it is important to get a horse that can help you develop. Bringing on a novice horse is not a job for a novice rider. Such a rider simply does not have the experience to help the horse on its journey. And that is really what we are talking about here, the transfer of experience. On this basis, I like to see novice riders with a horse around ten years old that has possibly jumped up to 1:20-1:30 metres. Always check the registration too. If the horse has had a lot of owners that would make me a little suspicious so make sure you do your homework. If the horse has come from abroad, again, check that all the necessary papers are in order.

Another tip is to not be fooled into thinking that a horse that has jumped at a higher level will accelerate your progress. You could purchase a Grade A horse and jump it at novice heights in the open competitions we have today. But the horse may well be sick of the sight of fences or might need a very experienced rider to get the best out of it. Doing this could also mask a lot of your own flaws and actually be detrimental to your development as a rider, leaving you pretty exposed when you jump off its back onto another horse.

Stay The Course

The goal of a showjumper is to jump clear rounds, it is that simple. To get to the jump off on your own, or as part of a team or even against the clock, the focus remains the same: Keep Going Clear! Therefore, it makes sense when you are buying a horse to see how it copes with jumping a full round with you on its back. Will this horse help me go clear at the level I am going to be competing at? Can it help me round the course? That is why, on your second visit, you need to put the horse through its paces and I would advise a good hour's schooling at this point too. Obviously horses will tire at different stages and at no point do you want to be jumping a tired horse, because that just leads to accidents. But you do want to understand where your horse's fitness levels are. If the horse is shattered after 15 minutes then there may be an underlying health issue. Make sure that your horse will help you stay the distance.

See The Vision

Finally, can you visualise success with the horse that you are about to buy? If you cannot visualise what success looks like and how you and your horse will achieve it then you are not ready to buy a horse, in my opinion. It all comes down to preparation and a clear understanding of where you are going and what is required to get there. Think of it like this:

You are offered £1000 to win a quiz. You are allowed to pick one person from your friends and family to help you. Instantly you will start evaluating your friends and family on their ability to help you win the £1000 prize. You will deliberate and evaluate and then arrive at the person you best think equipped to help you achieve the aim. This is not been based on who you love most, who makes you laugh hardest, who the prettiest is, who can run fastest or who is kindest. It is purely based on who you think has the most suited intelligence or knowledge to help you win. Therefore, you have seen the vision and chosen the partner most likely to help you realise your vision. The same applies when choosing your horse.

Now that you have identified the right horse for your abilities and development, the next most important thing is choosing the right tack and equipment. The following chapter looks at bridles, saddles and stirrups as well as the other equipment you might need.

3
Tack and Equipment

KEY POINTS

*Buying Tack − Saddles − Bridles & Bits −
Reins − Stirrups − Travel Equipment − Other Equipment −
Crops − Footwear (Horses & Riders) − Safety Equipment*

Buying Tack

Tack not only makes a difference between developing your jumping or not, it also helps you understand what you and your horse need. Although horse riding and showjumping are expensive pursuits, the most expensive tack is not necessarily the best. So seek advice from a number of trusted people before you commit to buying tack. Since your horse's performance depends on balance and your instruction through your hands, legs and feet, it is vital to ensure that you have the most appropriate tack to help you communicate clearly as well as ensuring both you and your partner's safety and comfort.

Saddles

Saddles are really all about common sense, but the trouble with common sense is that it is not very common. In the simplest terms, a saddle needs to fit properly, so, first things first, get your saddle fitted. Over the course of my career, saddlery has changed so much. Back in my competing days, I was my own saddle fitter and we would make do all the time. Using numnahs was as close to 'fitting' as we came. Today we have custom fitters that will ensure your saddle fits like a glove. They cost money, of course, but if you are in showjumping then it is not because you want to save money, that is for sure. It is a costly game so that is even more reason to ensure you get the essential parts right. Avoid falling into the 'one-way fit' trap either. Now, it is all well and good having your saddle fitted for your horse but you have to make sure that the saddle fits you too. If you are uncomfortable whilst riding it will show and it will also affect everything you do. Your control, balance, positioning, posture, weight distribution ... every single aspect, in some way, relies on your relationship with your saddle.

Make sure that your saddle is also a close contact saddle. By this I mean that there is not a huge amount of padding between your leg and the horse's side. The legs are often referred to as the accelerator but they are way more than that. They are your balance weights and your virtual umbilical cord to the horse. It is through the legs that I have connected with my horses and if you watch most top rider and horse combinations you will see the horse 'feel' their rider as much through the legs as they do through the reins.

It is also important to have good strong stirrup leathers and buckles, and there is a plethora of stirrups you can purchase these days. I would advise you to try a few and find what you feel most comfortable with.

Last but not least, make sure you check your girth because even if you have the best custom-made saddle in the world it is no use if it is facing the ground after one jump with you lying in a pile of dust. All in all, just make sure your saddle works for you and your horse. A good-fitting saddle to someone who wants to be a better showjumper is worth its weight in gold.

Bridles And Bits

My recommendation is to start with a snaffle bit on your bridle and see how it goes from there. A snaffle, which is one of the most common types of bit used while riding horses, consists of a bit mouthpiece with a ring on either side and acts using direct pressure. Keep the bridle high on the nose. I really do not like seeing them sitting low because I feel it inhibits the horse's performance and affects its breathing. Also, avoid over-tightening the bridle since it cuts out the wind coming in and out of the nose and stresses the horse.

There are a number of bits on the market which can do a good job, but a word of warning here on double bridles and bits. A double bridle fitted incorrectly is a dangerous weapon. It can destroy your relationship with your horse so get expert advice if you go for one of these. A Pelham bit, which is a half-moon shape and has a straight bar is good for a horse that you cannot hold. It has elements of both a curb bit and a snaffle bit. A curb bit is a more sympathetic bit than the Pelham due to its smaller action. It has D-rings at the side and works with leverage. Again, take advice on which bit is right for your horse, but I always tend to favour a snaffle because it is the kindest to the horse.

I once had a horse whose owner could not find the right bridle or bit for him. He had been to many shows and never made it over the first fence. I worked away with the horse, changed the bridle and made a few other tweaks. Over a short period of time he started to improve and you could feel how different his response was when ridden with the tack that best suited him. I took him to the Montrose show and he came fifth in his class. From there we qualified for the second round the following week and within a year he qualified for the Horse of the Year show. The horse was later sold for a lot of money and went on to win very big classes. I cannot say for sure that it was the bridle that changed the horse, but as I said, before the change he was stopping at the first fence. After the change, he competed at the highest level. Go figure!

Putting the correct bridle on a horse is not rocket science. It is more or less trial and error and I have never been frightened to try something different. You should become a specialist on tack and always try to see things from the horse's perspective. A foam rubber on the bridle for example can work well. If the horse has a mouth problem, it can still be a good horse, it just needs to be bridled correctly. Sometimes it is the very horse that someone else says is trouble or too much work that can give you the edge. I have never been a wealthy man so I relied heavily on seeing what was wrong with a horse, picking it up cheaply and schooling the fault out of them. For example, Trevarrion was a mare that came to me many years ago. She was going nowhere fast because she had a very sensitive mouth which needed light hands and lighter bridling. That horse went from a £250 washout to a multiple Grand Prix winner! You have to think like a horse. They need to be content. If they are not content, then they will not focus and if they are not focused you are in deep water. If they are content, then quite often the sky is the limit.

Obviously you want the horse to have the bit that suits its mouth. With some horses you can put a strong bit in them and they still pull against you. They can be very headstrong, as we know, and sometimes there is no alternative but to bit them strongly. However, it is very important to also change your feel and actions to the bridle and bit you are using. A strong bit requires light hands. You also need to monitor progress and not just keep the same bit for ages. Your goal should be to always use the lightest bit you can on your horse. I firmly believe that you want it to be as close to natural as possible. So if you put a strong bit or bridle on your horse make sure you constantly change it out as it develops. As the horse becomes better balanced, the bit and the reins should become lighter in your hands. It may well be the case that after a few sessions the horse has calmed down and therefore does not need the full regalia anymore. Stay sharp and do not be lazy. Aim for a light touch every time.

I have seen riders yank the bridle up until it pulls the sides of the horse's mouth and they think this works well. In my experience if a bit is too high on the horse's mouth it can rest on the horse's molar teeth. Make sure that the bit is sitting comfortably in the mouth. The horse has six teeth in the bottom of his mouth and then has its molars. The bars of its mouth are then situated in the middle and this is the area where the bit should go. When young horses are being broken, we put a mouthing bit in which has small weights called 'keys' fitted to it. The keys help harden the bars of the mouth so they are ready for stronger bits in the future, so keep an eye on this as a young horse that hasn't been broken correctly may have issues with the bit.

The great Irish rider Eddie Mackin is an excellent example of how to ride a horse with feel. He often rode Boomerang with a Hackamore and I remember people being constantly amazed at the fact he could control such a high-end horse with nothing more than a bitless bridle. What people did not take into consideration was that all the work had been done at home. Eddie is someone to look to when it comes to using bits and bridles correctly and I would encourage you to get on the internet and watch him in action.

Over-bitting is the scourge of showjumping. What often happens is that well-meaning but inexperienced parents want to make sure their child is safe when riding so they put on a bit on it that would stop an elephant. Take your time and get professional advice on how to bit your horse or pony. I have seen this so often in my teaching and it is one of the main recurring issues I face. And finally, do not be afraid to ask top riders for advice if you are a novice. They were once like you and good people will always try and help others. If they do not, then do not worry about that either. That is up to them. Just wait for the next one to come along and ask them.

Reins

I have always advised people to use a running martingale on a horse if they are going to jump because if you lose your balance the running martingale will keep the reins running no matter where you want to go. A bit and bridle without a running martingale can keep jarring a horse's head, and it takes special skill to keep the hands and balance required to maintain a good position. Many dressage and eventing people do not like martingales and I can understand their thinking in these disciplines, but for showjumping it is a running martingale every time for me. It gives you the best chance of recovery and consistent rein position.

When it comes to reins my preference was always rubber-covered reins as they gave me the best confidence in the wet and also if my hands were sweating. Nowadays a lot of riders wear gloves and I would do too if I were competing today. Whether they are rubber or a new synthetic material, the principle is the same and that is to ensure you have a rein that gives you the best possible control and grip. Practicality beats pretty almost every time. I would never jump in a double bridle at shows, though I know people who do. It is just my preference.

Stirrups

Nowadays, in addition to the trusted 'cheese graters', riders have magnets on the soles of their boots which fit onto magnets in the stirrups. In my day you were tied into the stirrups by string! However, the key is to keep your feet in the right position by focusing on what you are doing. I like to see riders using rubber-soled footwear with a few treads because you must make sure that you can get free easily. Make sure your stirrups are comfortable and meet your needs. Stirrups are important for balance and if the stirrup leathers are worn too long or too short your balance will be affected.

Try to buy good quality equipment. You do not want horses running away with broken head collars or ropes. Everything has to be done properly and maintained well. Your horsebox and trailer has to have enough room to move slightly and bend. Do not put your horse in so tight that standing against it is like standing up on a bus. They are not holding on – the horse has to keep its balance in a moving vehicle.

Travel Equipment

If you are going showjumping you need to anticipate and plan for the financial outlay. It is not a cheap sport, particularly when it comes to transport and travel equipment. You will soon start to realise that in order to take your horse from A to B safely you need to think seriously about travel. One thing that I am very passionate about is preparing your horse for travel. If you have a trailer or a wagon horsebox you need a proper rug in the box to stop the horse rubbing against the trailer. You also need to get some thick bandages to protect the horse's legs, although nowadays there are many different kinds of boots (these are often listed in the classified ads in horse magazines or on the internet). You also need to take hay, mix and feeding buckets and always take a shovel and brush with you because you have to sweep out your trailer and horsebox when you get to your destination. And do not forget to have plenty of fresh water. Horses drink a lot (up to 10 gallons a day) so make sure they do not dehydrate.

Other Equipment

If you can, you want to get your own jumping equipment. You will need a tack room to store all the equipment for saddles, cupboards for blankets, cupboards for bandages, boots etc. But do not panic if this is outside your budget. There are a number of yards around the country so never think that not having your own jumps and tack room are a barrier. Just cut your cloth accordingly. The only thing that matters is that you have access to the right facilities.

Crops

I am against any cruelty to horses. I hate to see it and I will never condone this type of behaviour. The use of crops attracts much controversy on the subject, but let us be clear here, crops do not hurt horses. People misusing crops hurts horses. In my opinion, a crop used correctly does not hurt a horse and can be a useful tool in managing the relationship between a horse and rider. Remember, a horse weighs about half a ton and it can toss you to the ground any time it feels like it. You have to be in charge in your relationship with a horse and sometimes they need a smack to smarten their ideas up. I know that a certain amount of people will disagree with this and that is their prerogative. However, I believe that crops used correctly actually help make showjumping safer.

Your first directive should be to not use your crop at all. A crop is not there to help you vent your frustration. It is there to keep your horse's focus on the job in hand. It is also important not to think that just restricting the force you use prevents cruelty. Be sure to only use it at the right time and on the right area of the horse (its rear quarters). Only use the crop when you are jumping if you absolutely have to. A horse can look backwards as easily as it can look forwards and if you distract it then its mind will not be on the job in hand. So use a crop, yes, but treat it with respect and use it for the purpose it is meant.

Footwear (Horses And Riders)

Horses in the big international competitions are now all wearing bigger, broader shoes. Back in my day the riders did not go to farriers – they went to the blacksmith. The blacksmith would measure the feet, take a shoe and fashion it to the size of the hoof and fit it to the horse's foot. This would cost four shillings and take a minimum of three hours. Now it is at least £100. In the army I spent time learning how to fit and drive shoes and trim the horse's feet. I used to shoe my own horses with my own driving hammer so I understand a bit about shoeing and this is always something I am happy to give advice on. Shoes are mostly concave iron with stud holes for the jumping horses. In some fields the grass might be newly cut and quite slippery on top, so the horse could lose its footing, since there is no depth of grass to keep them there. Now there are different surfaces but having the horse shod well is still key.

Boots can cost a fortune so makes sure you do your homework here. The best thing for children learning to jump is to get leather or rubber soled boots, gaters and chaps plus britches. And also, if you are going to ride at shows be mindful that jackets need to comply with the regulations too.

Safety Equipment

And finally in this chapter, make sure that you purchase the correct headgear and safety gear. Today we have fantastic equipment that really protects riders when they fall. Hats, body protectors, quick release catches, leg wraps; there is a multitude to choose from. Do not scrimp here either. You have one life and your health is of paramount importance. Be sensible and invest in your own safety.

4
Training And Schooling

Key Points

Good & Bad Days – Solo? No Go! – Fail To Prepare, Prepare To Fail – Horse Health Preparation – Your Horse's Mental Wellbeing – Physical Fitness – Tack Preparation – Schooling – Warming Up – Flat Work – Jumping – Speed

Training and schooling are the areas where you can really make a difference to your performance. When you get to the date of the competition it is too late to school your horse, or at least to school well. You have what you have at a competition and it is more about being prepared, staying focused and competing like an angelic demon. When you are training and schooling then you have the opportunity to develop both you and your horse in line with your vision. There are a number of key areas to concentrate on and I will take you through them in this chapter.

Good Days And Bad Days

This is just life; you have to be able to deal with this and factor it into your whole showjumping psyche. If you do not, you will end up eroding all the good work you have done and gravitating towards negativity, doubt, anger and a lack of confidence. These are all influences that will prevent you reaching you and your horse's potential. It is my belief that your horse is sensitive to your changing emotions so you have to be mindful of this. You will infect them too if you are at a low ebb. Frustration is, well, frustrating. It can influence so much of what we do so we have to be aware of it and channel it correctly. This is way easier to write about than to apply and we are all susceptible to emotions getting the better of us.

In 1988 I lost the livery stable that I had worked all my life to own. I had built it up through blood, sweat and tears and then lost it because I made some poor character judgements. At the time I had every emotion you could think of. I felt angry, I felt like a failure, I felt scared, I felt sorry for myself… my head was a mess. But in many ways, I wish that this had happened at the beginning and not the end of my career. It allowed me to do some soul searching and I realised that I had two choices. I could either let all these negative influences make my decisions for me or I could stay pragmatic and try my best to make positive choices from that day forward, and that is what I did. That is the key, I think, to why so many people like my teaching style.

What I realised is that you can blame others, you can blame yourself, you can blame whoever, but sometimes things just do not work out. However, there is always more to learn from failure than success. I focused on taking the positives, ditching the negatives and most importantly, moving on. Bitterness and grudges seldom hurt those you feel them for as much as they hurt you and those you love. So no matter whether you have stubbed your toe, had a fence down or lost the farm, move on because the only thing that is certain in showjumping, indeed, in life, is that some days are better than others. If you can truly understand this and place it in your mindset, what a weapon to have.

Make More Good Days Than Bad Days!

So if we can agree that we have good days' schooling and bad days' schooling then the task is simple. We need to try our best to ensure we have more good days than bad days and the best starting place is with our old friend, preparation. Do not think that schooling does not take the same preparation as competition, that you can just rock up when you are ready and jump on your horse's back. If you read the last sentence back again it sounds daft but plenty of people do it that way and expect to become world beaters. Preparation is the greatest friend you have when it comes to having more good days' schooling than bad ones. So how do we prepare?

Solo? No Go!

There are very few instructions in this book that I will categorically say must be followed. Interpretation is up to the individual and it is more important to have a concept in your head than follow it to the letter, but please, please, please do not school alone! It is crazy to do this! Showjumping carries real risk; we all know and accept this. But to add further risk, that is just not something I can condone. We can fall off and get hurt whether someone is there or not, true. However, the time it takes to receive medical attention after a fall or an accident is vitally important and if you are schooling on your own then the probability of receiving the necessary attention in the required time is significantly decreased. In short, you have less chance. This book is about doing all the things we can to become better showjumpers. Schooling on your own is simply not consistent with long-term development. So, please do not do it.

Fail To Prepare, Prepare To Fail

Let us say you are schooling tomorrow. Ask yourself this question: "Am I ready?" Have you set out what the plan is for the next day? Are the people you need support from briefed and ready? Is your horse ready? Do you have the equipment required? Clothing, tack, arena, fences – do not leave anything to chance. If you are prepared, then the chance of something bad happening is reduced and the chance of good things happening increases. My advice here is to use a checklist and tick things off. There is a suggested checklist in the appendix for you to customise and use. Remember to always self-evaluate each schooling session and this applies to how organised and prepared you are so that on the next occasion you school, you do not waste any precious time or money because you are not fully prepared. You can also develop the checklist for the skills and jumps you want to improve, sometimes with different horses.

After a while it will become second nature. Always keep your list to hand, because if you do reflect and learn from your experiences you can add things to the list to help you prepare, creating a 360-degree process of development through your own knowledge and understanding.

Horse Health Preparation

In my mind you should groom your horse every day. This is not just about making them look good, this is vital to your overall bond and it is essential in helping you know your partner and keeping them healthy and happy. In fact, if you have got a good rapport with your horse then they will often sense you coming or know the sound of your feet. They will also welcome the inspection too. You are looking for bumps and bruises, cuts and growths. You want to check their feet, their shoes, their legs and tendons. Feel if there is heat in the leg which often means it needs further examination. Be conscious of watching your horse and their reaction when you are checking them as quite often the horse will tell you if there is a problem by either pulling or shying away.

Remember, horses do not tell lies. You will never get a horse phoning in sick because he does not fancy going in to work that day or because he has been out on the hay the night before. When it comes to their health, in my experience, horses always tell the truth, but if you are not fully focused then you will not 'hear' them, so concentrate when you are checking them over. Your eyes and your hands are fantastic tools when it comes to keeping your horse healthy but only if they are sending signals to a knowledgeable and attentive brain. If you are fortunate enough to have a groom, make sure that they inform you of anything that they think could possibly be wrong and then it is up to you to take responsibility for the course of action from there. Grooms are there to assist but if you are the one that is going into the ring then you are accountable for the health of your horse.

Your Horse's Mental Wellbeing

In many ways, the physical side of checking your horse is the easy bit. The mental side is a little bit more difficult. If your horse is in a yard it may be very content for a long period of time and then boom, a new horse arrives and all hell breaks loose. Sometimes a new horse moving into a yard is never accepted but I have found this to be rare. Often after a period of time they will get to know each other and settle down. There is usually a hierarchy though and you have to be aware of this. There is no point in trying to force the issue in my experience. Better to simply respect the horses and integrate them slowly. More often than not I found that if you treat a horse with respect and no surprises, they will come around to your way of thinking.

Physical Fitness

Your horse needs to be physically fit if you are going to compete. The best way I found of keeping my horses fit was walking. Not doodling along the road but walking on, balanced in your hands and your leg on. In an ideal world, I would say it takes about six weeks to transform a horse from being a 'soft horse' (in other words from doing nothing) to a horse that is physically ready to compete. You have to build up their fitness over time and once you have done this you have to balance keeping them fit with not over-training them, which is an art in itself and very much dependent on your bond.

Feed is very important and just as we touched on with regard to your own physical performance, what you consume has a huge bearing on how you perform. The same is true when it comes to your horse. Today we have animal nutritionists and you can go to them and have your horse's feed designed specifically for them. Some think this is overkill but I believe that specialist knowledge really helps and that we simply cannot be the master of everything. Change and progress is inevitable and it is better to embrace it than fight it. You can bet your bottom dollar that none of the top horses in the world are eating random bowls of feed these days. Their food will be balanced and monitored daily with the optimum measures religiously adhered to. There is nothing to stop you doing exactly the same.

The health and fitness of your partner is essential and if you want to become a better showjumper then you have to treat your horse's health with the respect it deserves, so make sure you do a health check before you start schooling.

Tack Preparation

In the last chapter we went through the importance of tack and equipment. When you are preparing to school your horse, make sure your tack is ready. That is to say to make sure it is clean and fit for purpose. Check it over the night before and make sure that you have accounted for every piece of tack and equipment that you are going to need because time is precious; the last thing you want to be doing is running around on the day in a panic because you cannot find an important piece of your kit. It is a waste of everyone's time and it is counter-productive.

Schooling

As we mentioned earlier in this chapter, schooling all comes back to having a game plan, being focused and preparing in the right way to achieve your aims and vision. It is also the time to work on technique and this section now becomes more technical with regard to schooling. Competition is about adapting what you know to produce the best possible performance. As I touched on earlier, competitions are not the time to work on technique or try and develop your style simply because that part should have been done at home. Yes, you will learn things whilst competing but I always found that it is better to tinker around with things when you are schooling and that is what I teach to this day.

So, let us start with an indoor facility. You are heading to school your horse, so what is the first thing you need to be thinking about? The first thing for me is familiarisation. Even if this is your home yard, walk your horse gently round the arena a few times because it will give them the chance to get comfortable in the environment. You may have new jumps or painted the fences, laid a new surface with new smells; these can all spook a horse so just take it easy and let them gently take it all in before you do anything else. Do not take a single thing for granted because even the most placid horse can have a turn. Also be very careful if you have a new horse schooling with you, a mare in season or a stallion that knows there are mares in season. The horse you have known for years can change in an instant when primal instinct kicks in so be careful and plan your session sensibly.

Warming Up

This is not just about the horse. Before you mount, make sure you stretch yourself off. Jumping puts a huge strain on your body so if you are keeping fit and trying to improve your performance make sure you warm up before you get on your horse. If you are carrying knocks or aches and pains (and let us be honest, we probably all do more often than not) then it is important that we make sure we are as supple as we can be.

After walking your horse around the arena, pick up the reins tighter, put a little more leg on and ask the horse for canter, on the correct leg. That is to say, left is left, right is right. A nice easy way of doing this is to start your canter from the corners of the school as the natural angle and motion of a corner should help you find the stride with greater ease. Again, you do not want to fly in to anything so canter round the school a few times and stop and change legs a few times at the corners. Some horses are quite clever and will start to anticipate the change. My advice here is to go with it, as long as they are changing correctly. This should be another component part of your bond and if you do not have to work at going off on the correct leg, then that is great. However, most horses at novice level will need a wee bit of work and I cannot emphasise enough how important it is to get your horse travelling correctly before you do anything remotely close to jumping. If the horse does not go right on the flat, it will never go well over jumps and that leads nicely on to the area so many people neglect. Flat work.

Flat Work

Flat work is the bedrock of good showjumping and it is an area where good horsemanship really comes to the fore. What you want to achieve with flat work, primarily, is balance. A balanced horse needs to be tight between your legs and your hands. Not too tight but controlled and going forward in a manner that puts you in control and the horse feels like it is moving well and you are bonded. If you have a nervous horse, particularly concentrate on flat work. As I said, it is vitally important to go right on the flat because the movement and balance you have between jumps has a huge influence on how you will take off and land.

When I was schooling at home I focused on having my hands fixed in the middle so that the horse had something to hold on to with its mouth. So much about good riding is about creating good lines so try not to move your hands from side to side, sawing their mouth. Just sit tight and the horse will start to flex their neck, and when that happens tighten your hands a little, put a bit more leg on and ask them to walk on. If the horse complies then relax your hands and reward the horse right away with a good pat to the neck. Repeat this exercise, only this time instructing the horse to reverse. Flat work is not a five-minute exercise, but nor is it a five-hour exercise. To get your horse working well takes some real patience and effort but it is a worthwhile exercise, and when you get it right it is rewarding for you and your partner. I know it sounds boring but it is very satisfying and the benefits to both of you are huge. You will see a lot of top class riders do this before they start a class. It is all about getting the focus, muscle memory, balance and bond aligned through control and feel.

On the track round the school, put a pole out and let your horse trot over it a few times. They might not like the colour or shape. Stop them at this point, reassure them, pat them on the neck then go again. They might take fright so do not take the pole away or change it for a different colour, because invariably they will have to jump that particular colour at some point so you may as well overcome this challenge today. Just be gentle and reassuring. If they are really struggling and you have a schooling partner with you, then have them take their horse over the pole in front of yours because, as we discussed earlier in the book, this can help. Once you manage to get them going over the pole introduce another pole approximately seven feet away and repeat the routine.

Add another pole the same distance away from the second, repeat and then add a fourth, again the same distance from the third and repeat. Once you have the four poles evenly spaced and your horse is trotting through them, repeat this about eight to twelve times, trying to keep a straight line through the middle of the poles each time. You should be relaxed, hands at the neck, sitting up and allowing the horse to move forward. Once complete, give your horse a good rewarding pat again and make a fuss of them. Horses know when they have done well and like most of us, we respond much better when we are praised for doing well.

At this point, I would advise taking your horse out of the school. This may puzzle you a little but bare with me. What we are trying to achieve here is relaxation. It is almost like having a coffee break at work. Just a few minutes' walk then back to the school. This not only relaxes your horse but it also allows you to take them out and back in to the school, which helps them prepare for competition.

Once you are back in the school, pick them up again, balance, rein back and then trot through the poles once more. If your horse trots through the poles well, reward with the usual pat and then get your support guys to make the poles approximately 3 metres apart. Use part of the school for a canter area with no poles, then come around from there and canter through the poles again. If you are satisfied, reward again, then bring in your wings to the end of the fourth pole and make a cross pole with the ends about 30cm in height and let your horse come through there. The poles on the ground before the jump will control your pace. Do this a few times and then if this is a new horse to you, a young horse or a horse lacking fitness, that will do for that day. Take them for a few miles' hack then put them away. Job's a good 'un! You do not want to sicken your horse and you have to ensure that you build up slowly.

Once your horse is doing this exercise with ease then it is time to school on a bit. We are talking about taking an hour to do the above correctly in the beginning. As you go forward it will take less and less time, and when you are confident and prepared it should take only 20 minutes before you are ready to go jumping. However, if your horse is more experienced, fit and capable, then attempt some jumps if you like, but be honest and do not try and be a hero.

Jumping

There are a number of exercises I use in my training to develop techniques for jumping. Again, for your convenience, I have put a table in the appendix for this chapter at the end of the book for you to take out with you when you are schooling to practice these exercises.

I was always one of those riders who managed to keep their confidence as the fences were raised. I sometimes wonder whether this was bravery or stupidity but to be serious I think it was down to the fact I was always prepared and focused. A lot of people put up fences so big that their horses are frightened of them. Do not fall into this trap. Put up realistic sized fences consistent with the heights you will be jumping. Nowadays, there are so many different novice competitions with varying height restrictions so you are not allowed to have a fence any higher than the fences you will be jumping in competition. Do not faze yourself or your horse.

My advice to someone who is starting to compete is to believe yourself and also to not feel daunted. If you do not have the confidence or have second thoughts about a jump, stop. Think about it. Be honest with yourself and believe me when I say there is no shame in deciding to leave it for another day. Let me tell you, it often takes way more courage to decide not to jump than to jump. Get back to schooling, maintain your focus and keep practising until you are ready. Start at home with fences lower than the one that you do not yet have the confidence for. Then just raise the jump one pole at a time and once your horse has jumped and you are happy with that, do not go higher than that. After you have built up mutual confidence and trust with your horse, then you can keep going, but only try a small rise at a time.

Speed
When I started out there was no such thing as a clock. We would have a judge and six or seven fences which were built by non-officials who, let's just say, had better intentions than abilities. When you jumped there were four faults if the horse hit the fence with the front legs and two faults if the back legs hit it. At the end of the first round those who had jumped clear could jump again, only the fences were then raised higher. There were no course builders as we know them now. Instead some well intentioned soul would take charge and build the course. It was all about jumping clear. Then the clock came in and the judge had a stopwatch but the rider could not see the clock. Nowadays there is a beam and the horse goes through it and breaks it to starts the clock. The horse breaks the beam again for the digital clock to stop. It is only in recent years that riders have actually been able to see the clocks as they are jumping.

My advice to riders who have been competing for a while but want to get their speed up is, firstly, you can only go as fast as the course allows. Whilst planning the course you can see exactly where you want to go and how to cut off a few corners, to save some time. However, you also want to establish where the best point is to turn into the corners and also where you can possibly take a stride out because that is very important in the jump off. My advice to novices is try to keep within the time allowed and focus on going clear. In many ways, forget the clock. Just make sure you are focused and you jump a 'tidy' round. If you do not win, that is okay. You are a novice going clear in a jump off. That is real progress and your salad or fish supper, depending on whether you took my advice earlier, will taste very nice on the way home.

When I schooled my horses, I trained them to jump at an angle across the jumps for speed but, again, do not do that unless you have someone experienced with you because it can go wrong. If you are a more experienced jumper then being able to go across a fence at an angle is a very valuable skill. Riders need to be balanced and you have to plan the angles well because if you do not, you may find that you save a second at one fence only to add two seconds at the next one. Remember to see the whole course. Every angle has to fit the next one. It is all about smooth, progressive lines. You will gain way more time that way.

On a right-handed jump you communicate through the right leg when coming to and going over the fence so as to land the horse on the other leg. The rider shifts their balance so the horse's balance shifts too. If you have done the job properly then he will land on the right leg and move forward efficiently. Scott Brash is a master at this so watch him in action if you get the chance. During any jump you are communicating the direction with your horse by feel and weight distribution but even the slightest shift in balance can have an effect so do not be lazy. Your posture and position guides a horse and if you focus on this and work hard at it you will see results.

Being good against the clock is about being able to jump the course economically. That is to say, you should use the least amount of ground possible. It is also about having great imagination. These are the two main factors. Of course your horse benefits from being fast but I have seen many speedsters clatter fences because they get beyond themselves. Essentially, it is about seeing the lines that allow you to navigate the course in the most efficient way and in the least number of strides possible. Speed is more than going fast. Speed is also preparation, vision and heart.

I absolutely believe that these training and schooling tips will help develop you and your horse's jumping ability. They have worked time and again for me and I have seen many of the top riders use them to great effect. In the next chapter we will put it all together and look in more depth at competing.

5
Jumping And Competition

Key Points

Manage Your Time – Know Your Schedule – Prepare For Change – Bond – Be Smartly Dressed – Plan The Course – Find Your Switch – Jump To Win – Winning – Criticism To The Head, Praise To The Heart – Manage Your Brand

When it comes to competing you have to be single minded and focused. If you are there to make up the numbers then fair play to you, it is your prerogative to do that and I wish you well. However, winning is a great feeling and I would urge everyone who decides to compete to try to win. Channelled correctly, the desire to win can provide great enjoyment and satisfaction. It is not about gaining dominion over others or being able to brag. That just shows up your own insecurities and lack of humility; if you have witnessed this from others before then you will know how it made you feel. It is not an attractive quality.

Winning for me was about self-satisfaction. It was proof positive that all the things I was working on whilst training and schooling were having a great influence on my own ability and equally importantly, my horse's ability. I also liked the fact that winning showed I could handle the pressure. Believe me, I got nervous before every class but I always tried to channel my nerves into excitement. I like to think that it did in fact help me to stay humble. Many times I would use it to remind me that I was at a horse show, with a great horse, competing in the sport I loved with some genuinely nice people around me. What is there to be nervous about? Get out there and do the thing you love doing. Do not worry about falling off. Everyone has fallen off at some point. Focus on going well. Focus on what you can do, rather than what you cannot.

Did it work? Most of the time, yes. Did I fall off sometimes? Absolutely. It is how you get back on that counts.

So where is the beginning of competition? It is a moot point and you could debate it all day. For me we are always training and schooling for competition. It might be a year away, it might be a week away, but if you want to be a better showjumper then it is the moment you decide to compete. The previous chapter hopefully addressed some key points that I believe you will benefit from when it comes to preparing to compete. So in this chapter I am going to look at how we perform on the day of competition.

Manage Your Time

If you are rushing around on the morning of the competition, then you are already putting yourself at a disadvantage. If the show is a good distance away, go the night before. This takes out any possible traffic and other logistical challenges. If you cannot travel the night before then leave in plenty of time on the day. If this means going to bed at 7pm the night before, do it. This is a simple part of the competition that is in your control. Control it.

Know Your Schedule

It is imperative that you manage your schedule well and that you know it inside out. Most likely you will have a support team of some sort with you but they are there for support, not to mollycoddle you. Take responsibility because it is you, not them, who will be in the ring.

Prepare for Change

Inevitably, schedules do change. This will impact on your preparation and often invites stressful behaviours. Do not stress! Stress will wreck your plans, nothing surer. Be smart. Listen to the changes. Absorb them, regroup and refocus.

Bond

If you are feeling nervous then just think how your horse feels. New surroundings, new smells, new horses… it is all different for them. It is therefore important to get your bond working right away. Do not neglect your partner. Spend time with them, calm them, reassure them, get them as familiar as possible to their surroundings. The more you steady their nerves, the more chance you have of performing well.

Be Smartly Dressed

Showjumping has never had more of a connection with fashion than it has today. To be honest, I love it. If you want to be successful, dress successfully. It feels good when you are smartly dressed. So enjoy it. This is a small but important part of competing. If you are not well turned-out, then chances are you have not prepared as well as you could have. I learned this in the army and believe to this day that it has a positive affect on your overall performance.

Plan The Course

Please do not use the phrase 'walking the course' anymore. It is not correct. You need to plan the course. So often I see people chatting away as they walk round, learning very little. Either that or they are too focused on strides and they miss everything else, or worse still, they follow the person they admire most and try to second guess what is in their thoughts. Unless you are a mind-reader, that is not an intelligent strategy. But before you even walk it, if there is a grandstand then sit up there for a wee bit and look down on the course. Make notes and go over them in your head. Look for lines that join together to make a smooth round. Also establish areas where you could sort your stride if it goes wrong. Take it all in. Then, when it comes to actually going round the course, have a plan. When I walked round a course I wanted to know exactly where I would be positioning myself. I wanted to know the distance in-between the fences on trebles and doubles. This is the most important part of distance evaluation as there is very little room for error once you are in there. And use your walking paces, not other people's. You should have your horse's stride etched in your brain. How often at home do you check that the stride you use matches your horse's actual stride? If the answer is not often then make sure you do. It is pointless striding about the ring unless you know this.

Also remember as part of your course planning that different jumps require different approaches. For example, if it is a high upright then a very casual approach is often needed. A parallel jump needs more speed.

I also liked to connect the fences in some way and jumped the course a number of times in my head. I think it is good to visualise what you are about to do. It is crazy to work hard at home and then mess up because you have jumped the wrong fence. Another important point here is to make sure you understand the rules. If

1935: This is my mother, Esther, and I in Woodhouse Street, Knightswood, Glasgow. My father, Arthur, had purchased the kilt outfit at the famous 'Barras' market in the Gallowgate. It cost him the princely sum of 5 shillings (25p)!

1935: Around the same time, a young showjumper was making waves throughout the German equestrian scene. His name was Otto Klitzke. Little did I know then what a profound effect he would have on my life. If you look closely in this photo you will see a weight cloth under his saddle. Each horse in those days had to carry the same weight.

1945: Garscube Estate, Bearsden, Glasgow (where the Glasgow School of Veterinary Medicine is now) was the venue for the Welcome Home Horse Show Fundraiser for Soldiers, Sailors and Airmen. Showjumping was a 'new thing' to many people and it was at this show that I had my first taste of serious competition. I was about 17 years old and my horse was called Cutty Sark.

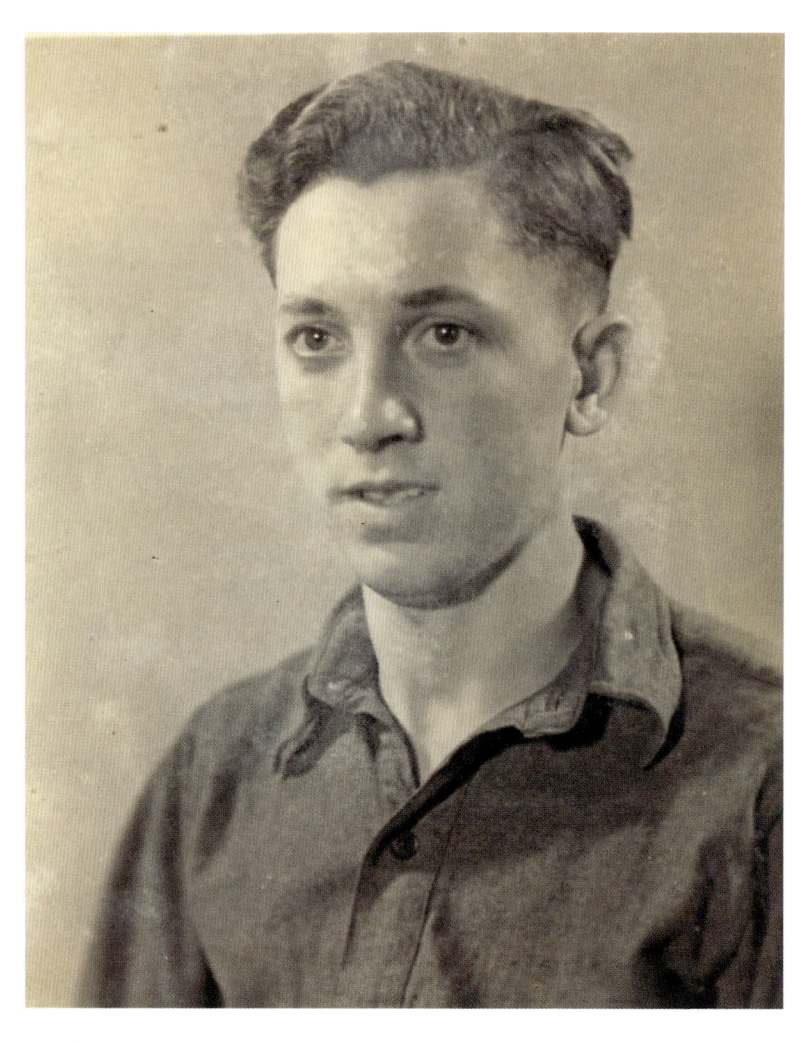

1947: In February I was called up for National Service. We were kept in the barracks in Litchfield, Staffordshire for over a week until we could walk properly and salute an officer correctly. We had no idea where we would be posted and as fate would have it I was sent to Berlin.

1947: Berlin. I find myself in charge of the stables at the Olympic Stadium. In German it is called the Reitanlage Olympiastadion, I recall. We referred to it as Glockenturm (The Belfry), which was the nearby street named after the the stadium's clock tower. In this picture I am posing with two soldiers who had come to learn more about riding out. I have always had a great love for dogs and it seems that the feeling is mutual here too.

1947: An Italian mare called Pat that I grew very fond of. This is in the yard at Glockenturm and if you look carefully you can see the hitching rail on the left. This was used to tie the horses up in the morning for inspection. I think there were approximately 20 horses stabled there at the time.

1947: There is a beautiful woodland area near Glockenturm called the Grunewald where we would exercise the horses. It was a peaceful, pleasant place to ride out for horses and riders, although I do not look too pleased to be getting my photo taken here!

1947: Pat and I getting ready to go out on parade. The tack is full military order and the blanket underneath the saddle had two roles: help the saddle fit and provide warmth to the soldier if needed at night. The bridle is a head collar and bridle combined. This allowed me to remove the bit and reins when I tied the horse up.

1947: Pat and I clearing the water jump at the outdoor arena in Glockenturm, for the first time! I remember that she jumped it really well. She was as honest as the day is long. A very special little horse. Note Otto sitting by the bush in the background.

1947: Myself and an unnamed horse that was sent to the remount station at Hanover. Remount was where the horses were stabled after the war before being redistributed around the country. The man in the white jacket is none other than Herr Von Korus, the Glockenturm riding instructor.

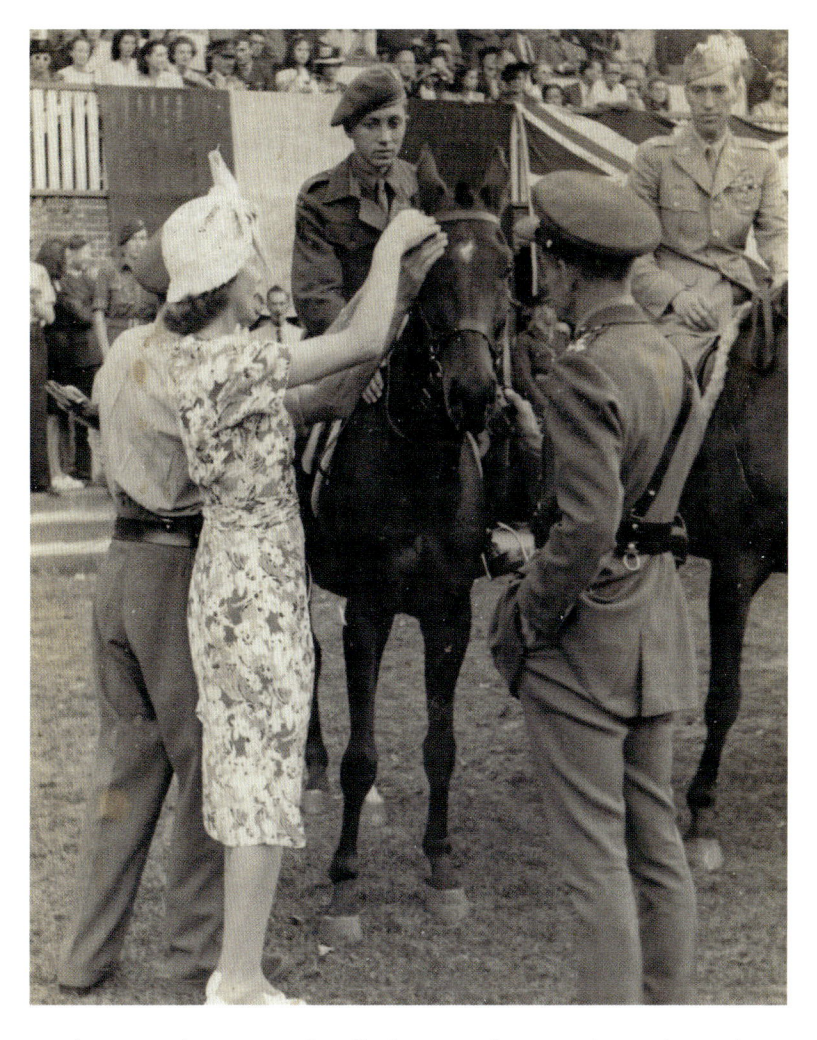

1947: Pat and I winning the Allied Forces Championship at the outdoor arena in Glockenturm. To the extreme right is Col. Kaiser, a real gentleman and a super rider from the US Army. Pinning on the rosette is the lady I mention in the book.

1947: Don't be fooled by the frowning face, I was overjoyed with the win. The three children in the background were horse daft and they treated me like a celebrity for a while.

In **1948** we moved the horses to Spandau, Berlin for the winter. This picture is at the American Sector. Even back then they had all weather surfaces, a luxury I had to wait a number of years for in the UK. The horse I am riding was called Effendi, an East Prussian gelding.

1948: Otto Klitzke at Spandau, Berlin. The building in the background was a huge, fantastically equipped indoor school which I believe was used before the war by a German cavalry regiment.

1948: A rare afternoon off! Yours truly posing for a photo at my friend's flat in Berlin. The area was referred to as the 'married quarters' as the houses were allocated to couples serving in the forces.

1948: Having a fly smoke before heading out on vehicle patrol. Smoking was commonplace in those days but I am pleased to say that I later quit the habit.

1948: Gatow Airfield Show, Berlin. Effendi and I tackling a fence that was more cross-country than showjumping. I seem to recall there was horse racing there that day too.

1948: Copche and I going through our paces at Spandau, Berlin. Copche, a little cob, was an outstanding six bar jumper, the best I've ever ridden, in fact. He could not jump a normal course to save his life though. He simply lost concentration.

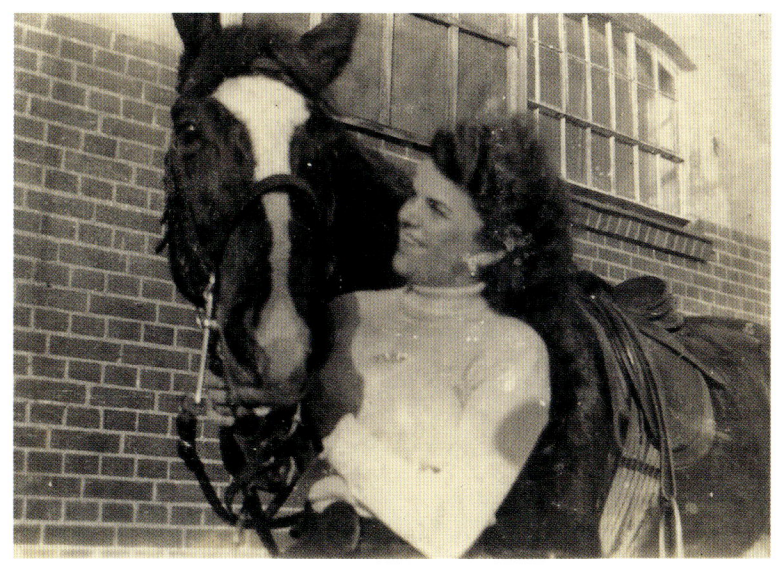

1948: Otto Klitzke's daughter, Inga. She was a superb horsewoman and a lovely girl too.

1948: The Best Rider Competition was run by the American Riding Association in Berlin. I managed to win the event by being able to do a figure of eight with no hands. Effendi was a good partner for me. I also remember that the chap who was third was not amused at all at losing.

1953: Gib Ralston, a gentleman and a good friend, and I 'showing the horse the fence' as part of our planning of the course. This was how we used to do it back in the day. Note the headgear of choice. Not too much protection there! Health and Safety would have had a field day. We looked the part though.

1953: My dear departed wife Marjory. She was definitely the brains of the outfit and not really a horsey person. She put up with a lot from me and supported the family so well as I travelled around the country. She was the backbone of my whole career and I miss her every single day.

1953: Jumping a sectional wall at Campsie Show, Lennoxtown, Glasgow on Glencoe. This was primarily an agricultural show that showjumping was introduced in to. The jumps used to travel round from show to show in those days, privately owned by Alex Pirie, I think.

1953: Practice time at my riding school in Bearsden, Glasgow on Glen Douglas. The fence was actually made from banana boxes from the fruit market in Candleriggs, Glasgow.

1953: The Field Riding School, Bearsden, Glasgow. I was very proud of this business and this picture was actually taken by my wife Marjory. The horse on my right shoulder was hit by a car on the Stockiemuir Road and had to be put to sleep. It was a sad day and another example of why we need to work even harder to make our roads safer to ride on.

1955: Campsie Show, Campsie Glen, Glasgow jumping a very dangerous looking hedge fence. This was in the days before we had course builders or designers. Note how Shadow, my horse, has come right in to the bottom of the jump because it is positioned the wrong way.

1961: Marjory and I getting married at New Kilpatrick Church in Manse Road, Bearsden, Glasgow on the 26th of December 1961. Without a doubt one of the happiest days of my life.

```
              THE MARE'S 'TAIL'.


        I saw a boy some years ago,
           A-riding on a handsome bay,
        We smiled and nodded for a week,
           Before he went upon his way.

        He left me with romantic dreams,
           Of riding always by his side,
        Of smiling up into his face,
           And he the groom and I the bride.

        In later years again we met,
           And dreams became reality,
        But when he jumped down from his horse,
           He was not tall - but rather wee!
        And as for travelling by his side,
           Alas - I had no nerve to ride.

        But share his life I did for sure,
           And groomed his horse and spread manure,
        Learned to drive and make a mash,
           And cook a meal by calor gas,
        Clean a saddle and make a halter,
           See him thrown and never falter,
        And rise at dawn to get things done,
           To please my love my chosen one.

        But now it seems I've passed my test,
           He's popped the question and I've answered yes,
        The steading's ready with hay and straw,
           And horses and dogs and a' and a'.


        And so good friends if you ever feel able,
           Your welcome tae the muckin'
        O' Willie's stable!

                  ---oOo---
```

1961: Marjory's poem that she read out at our wedding reception. Brings tears and smiles to my face every time I read it.

1962: Taken at a show just off Alexander Parade in Glasgow. The horse was called St John and he went so well that the owner sold him that day! Marjory loved Yorkshire Terriers and this one was called Bonnie.

1962: At the Haycock Hotel, Wansford, Cambridgeshire. It was a two day journey to Hickstead at that time. In this picture I am joined by my horse Toryhill and my German Sheperd Toscar. I qualified 'Tory' for the Foxhunter but unfortunately he was sold before I had the chance to ride him there.

1963: For the life of me I cannot remember the name of this horse but it is definitely jumping at the Royal Lancashire Show in Stanley Park, Blackpool. This was the first time I ever met showjumping legend Curley Baird. His brother Don held the high jump record for many years.

1963: Auchengreoch Farm near Howwood, Renfrewshire with my wife Marjory's favourite Vauxhall parked at the door. The horse, a pure Connemara, and foal belonged to Elizabeth Campbell who kept her horses with me at the time.

1964: Again at Auchengreoch Farm, this is a foal I bred that actually went on to become a jump racehorse. It did not set the heather on fire as a racehorse so we took it back and turned it into a good showjumper. It was called Iande, an anagram of my daughter Diane's name.

1965: Brimista was one of the best horses I ever had. She had been a racehorse and I am led to believe that she once held the track record for five furlongs at Hamilton. She had a brilliant spring, was brave as a lion and was quick over the ground. The horse in the background is Trevarrion who was an outstanding horse too.

c.1968: Receiving the winners rosette at Overhailes, Midlothian. The horse was Jane Eyre and this was the first time I ever rode her. She had been stopping a lot previously but she was brilliant for me that day. I rode her a week later at Barskimming, Ayrshire where she won again. From there the owner, Basil Walker, took her to Yorkshire and sold her on.

1968: Taken at Forres Show in Morayshire. Pat Rodger, far left of picture, won the class. I was second, David Reid from Broughty Ferry was third and the lady on the far right of picture, who was fourth, is none other than Lorna Sutherland (Clarke). The horse she is on is the famous Popadom who won Burghley in the late 1960s.

c.1968: Trevarrion winning the B&C at Ayr County Show, Ayrshire. She was fourth or fifth in the Foxhunter the day before. The weather was appalling but we managed to power through. I knew early on that she was going to be a phenomenal jumper.

1968: Treavarrion at Garscube Show, Bearsden, Glasgow. You can see she was still quite green given the height she is over the fence. Aileen Ross bought her from Archie Murdoch (whom I rode her for) and then she was sold on to the Gascoigne family and ridden by Malcolm Pyrah.

c.1971: Ramble On and I at the Bonnyrigg and Lasswade Show, Midlothian. This was a super event, held just after the Royal Highland Show. Competitors were always treated very well and I have fond memories of this show. (Photo by kind permission of P. M. Gray)

c.1971: Taken in the field that was to becoming my jumping paddock at Dykehead Farm, Darvel, Ayrshire. This picture shows Ramble On being ridden by a Swedish girl who was interested in buying him. You can see the owner, Peter Irvine, and I willing the horse over in the background.

c.1972: Big John jumping at Stonehouse Show in Lanarkshire. This was his first time at a show with me and he jumped well. Stonehouse was quite close to me when I stayed in Ayrshire and we enjoyed nipping over 'the border' and competing there.

c.1973: This good-looking boy is Softy Junior. He was brought to me after he just gave up trying. I managed to get him going again but he always had a habit of losing interest every so often. When he was interested though he was a very good horse, seen here on his way to winning the Foxhunter Regional Final at the Royal Highland Show, Ingilston, Edinburgh.

c.1973: Softy Junior picking up first prize for the same class. On the right is Simon Rodgerson, who was second the year before. I was third that year. Unfortunately out of shot is Rita Birch, who won the event the year previous and was third in this class. Both were great competitors and lovely people.

1974: My daughter Diane and I with her pony Angus. Diane was the talented rider out of my children and competed well in ponies. However when she grew out of ponies she did not want to go into horses and I was fine with that. It is important to let people make their own decisions, especially your children.

1975: St Corry and I at the Horse of the Year Show, Wembley Arena, London in the final of the Foxhunter Championship. This is the first fence in the first round, or the warm up stakes as it was called. St Corry was jumping well and after the morning round I knew I had a chance.

1975: This is St Corry and I in the Foxhunter Final jump off and really flying after a slow start. Again, look at how focused she is. She was a winner and if you are ever looking for a horse, this is the kind of focus you want to see when it is in action.

1975: What I like about this picture of St Corry and I in the Foxhunter Final is that she is tucked up well and paying attention, ears pricked forward. She actually never touched a fence from the regional final right the way through. She did not like warming up though, in fact she hated it. She only ever switched on in competition.

1975: Without a doubt the highlight of my jumping career. The Foxhunter is the competition that all riders with novice horses want to win. I could not have been prouder and I can still recall the rounds I jumped to this day. Special memories. (Photo by kind permission of Clive Hiles)

```
                              17 Overdale Gardens,
                                 GLASGOW, G42 9QG,
                                    8.10.75.
    Dear Mr. Sheret,

                      Congratulations on your
    great achievement on winning the most coveted
    prize at Wembley, the one which attracts
    thousands of entries all over the country

                      At Ingliston, an American
    Student who competes in show jumping in Texas
    greatly admired your competence and the way in
    which you guided your horses skilfully and
    considerately, without any fuss.

                      Mr. Sheret does a great deal
    to keep Scotland in the forefront of show
    jumping and to ensure that the spectators
    always have an interesting and educative
    day when he is competing.

                      I think you must hold the
    Scottish record for the number of entries in
    Scottish Shows in a Season!

              Mit herzlichsten Grüssen,

                      Robert R. Takahira
```

1975: Robert Takahira was an academic who came to many shows during my competition days. He was a well-liked, softly spoken gentleman who used to ask you politely if he could give your horse a mint; maybe that is where I got my mint fetish? He wrote this lovely letter to me after I won the Foxhunter with St Corry. It reminds me when I read it that the smallest of things can often carry the most value.

1975: Back home at Dykehead Farm, Darvel, Ayrshire with my three children Diane, David and Gavin. Looking back on my career I sacrificed a lot of time away from my family so moments like these were precious.

1976: My son David was a reluctant horseman. Contrary to what he says, he was a good rider. Here he is with my daughter Diane and Angus at Strathaven Show, Lanarkshire in the Fancy Dress Competition. Not quite sure what the thinking was behind the outfit but it was a fun family day.

1976: Logie and I at the Horse of the Year Show, Wembley Arena, London in the Grade C Championship. The horse was owned by my dear friend Tommy Brewster and I can remember how nervous he was that night. I think we managed a respectable fourth place. I recall that the great Caroline Bradley won the class that night on Tigre.

1977: The Horse of the Year Show, Wembley Arena, London, on Brimista. Unfortunately she picked up an injury on her back leg that night which she never recovered from. I was heartbroken when the vet put her to sleep. She was an outstanding horse and my friend.

c.1977: Raising funds for the Riding for the Disabled Charity in Newmilns, Ayrshire. The Rotary Club organised the event and Diane and I were only too keen to get involved. Marshall Law is my mount and Diane is on the trusty Angus.

c.1978: This was at Bigger Show riding an Irish horse whose name escapes me. I only had her for a week and then she was away. Bigger is in South Lanarkshire and the show became a favourite for the Scottish showjumpers for a while. George Nimmo, a great Scottish showjumping stalwart, was the local hero there.

c.1978: Carnwath Show, Lanarkshire was another great and well attended show. This triple bar was about a 5 foot spread and maybe 4 feet high. I always tried to make sure I had a little more pace going into a triple bar and also that the horse was taken right in to the bottom of the jump.

c.1978: Ricky Pearson's Marshall Law and I jumping for fun on very heavy ground at Coatbridge Show, Lanarkshire. On heavy ground you have to be even more steady and precise. Forget tight turns and riding flat out. Just keep your horse safe and go clear.

c.1978: Another triple bar but this time at Lanark Show, Lanarkshire. The show was held in the centre of the race course and the track was always good. I enjoyed jumping there and won many a class, including the Foxhunter.

c.1978: Diane and I at the children's meet of the Lanark and Renfrewshire Hunt, Bowfield Country Club, Howwood, Renfrewshire. Her pony was called Steppings Merry Overture and I bought it from Mrs McCorkindale who owned Dales of Dalry. It was a cracking little pony and looked after Diane well that day.

c.1979: Jumping at Peebles Show. My horse had a knee pad on as it had developed a little injury earlier. Nothing too bad but I wanted to give it a little extra protection. Peebles is in the Scottish Borders and home of Olympic Gold Medalist and former World Number One Scott Brash MBE, who would have been about 6 years old when this was taken.

c.1979: Proudly searched on Tayinloan. I named the horse after the small Argyll village that we used to spend caravan holidays at each year. He was a bit of a rascal to be honest but I spent a good bit of time schooling him and we ended up getting along fine.

c.1980: Drymen Show on Sir Hugh Fraser's Arthur of Troy. What a horse he was! Arthur was bought from Trevor Banks, who I think bought him from Princess Anne. He always wanted to win and in the beginning he would jump too high. But he settled down and was without doubt one of the very best I ever rode. (Photo by kind permission of Photoflash)

c.1980: On Chef d'Equipe duties at Muirmill, Ayrshire with the 14'2 Scottish Team competing in the Home International. It was a great honour and thankfully the team ended up victorious. I seem to remember that the 12'2 and the 13'2 teams also won. A good day for the Scots.

c.1980: This photo brings back very happy memories. On the left is George Nimmo. He was a great character and there was always a devilish wit in his eyes. He is also, for you younger readers, Scottish showjumper Mark Turnbull's grandfather. The lady in the middle is the lovely Isabel Black who went on to become Mrs Isabel Mcgeoch.

c.1980: Talk about a rouges' gallery. On the left is my groom at the time, Kathleen Young. A really nice, hardworking girl and wild as the heather. Next to her are my friends Bill McFarlane, Ricky Pearson and Billy Stewart, with me in the background. Taken at the Royal Highland Show, I think.

1980: Training in Banff, Alberta, Canada. The horse belonged to a lovely Canadian chap called Ray Green who had invited me over for a month to run clinics there. I loved Alberta, such a beautiful province. You can see here that I have draw reins on the horse as it was throwing his head in the air a lot.

c1982: The late Ricky Pearson and I at East Gavin, Howwood, Renfrewshire. Ricky was taken from Liz and his girls Clare and Jill way too young. He was one of the best friends I have ever had. Funny, smart, generous and sharp as a tack.

c.1982: Newmilns Show was our local show when I started in Ayrshire. They used to hold it at Downiesburn Park which sat alongside the River Irvine. The show had a great atmosphere and I always tried to attend and support it if I could.

c.1982: Presenting John Brown with the Regional Final Foxhunter Championship at Jumps in Carluke, Lanarkshire. John was a fantastic talent in his competing days in Scotland and someone I greatly admire as a showjumper and a horseman. I never realised I looked so much like a mad scientist back then!

c. 1983: Jumping at Ayr County Show on Ricky Pearson's Marshall Law. Ayr was and is a great show. I remember winning a class there on Arthur of Troy. It was a speed class and Sir Hugh Fraser had told me the trophy would look very nice on his mother's piano. So I obliged as every sensible rider does and I jumped a two-stride double in one stride, that was Arthur's forte. Always good to keep the owners happy.

1984: Back at the jumping paddock at Dykehead Farm, Darvel, Ayrshire with Quando. What a great horse he was! That gate is four feet high alone. I do not think I had more pleasure training a horse than Quando. He was a star.

c.1986: Gleneagles, Perthshire was the venue here. Sean Connery had been asked to present us with our prize. He has been a favourite actor of mine for many years so it was nice to meet him in person.

c.1989: In the last few years of my working life I worked at Pollock Park looking after the heavy horse teams. These boys I think were from Glasgow Green and I was helping them out for the day. Clydesdales and Shires are magnificent animals and I never need calling twice to work with them.

c.1990: My great friend Jim Leitch and I have always had a passion for carriage driving. This is us with Sally in Bearsden helping promote the arts. I am not too sure what it had to do with carriage driving but Jim and I never needed much of an excuse to yoke up!

1990: Opening meet of the Lanark and Renfrewshire Hunt at Houston House with a very young and smiley Blythe Brewster. Her Dad Tommy can be seen on the extreme left of the picture talking away to our friend Archie Stewart, who is now sadly no longer with us.

2013: Twenty-three years on and here is Tommy, Blythe and I again. Tommy Brewster was without doubt one of the best horsemen I knew. He passed away in the autumn of 2015 and he is sadly missed. A true gentleman.

1993: Harrowing the field at Pollock Park. This was actually my last day before I retired. The boys doing the work are Rocky, right, and Ranger. Rocky was a Clydesdale/Shire cross and Ranger was a Shire. They were brilliant horses and it was sad to say goodbye to them.

1993: A mare and her yearling foal at Pollock Park. The mare was from Linn Park in Glasgow and they had asked me to look after her when she was put in foal during my time working there.

1998: I can not help but feel sad when I look at this picture. I am on Ann Williamson's Ashen Prince at Chatelherault Country Park, near Hamilton, Lanarkshire. This is the last time I ever competed as a showjumper. We all have to stop sometime and I knew that day that it was time to call time. I was fortunate that I managed to compete until I was 70 years of age. But it is never an easy thing to walk away from something you love. So my advice here is compete for as long as you can and do not forget to enjoy every moment along the way.

2003: My son David commissioned the late, great Aberdeen artist Eric Auld to paint this for me. I was thrilled to receive such a nice gift and it now hangs resplendently in my hall at home.

2005: Myself and my daughter Diane with two bouncers, sorry, Beefeaters in the courtyard at Buckingham Palace. They were lovely fellows and added great colour to this picture.

2005: One of the proudest days of my life. Collecting an MBE for Services to Showjumping in Scotland from HRH Queen Elizabeth II. A real honour and one I share with every Scottish showjumper of all levels. (Photo by kind permission of BCA Film.)

2005: Standing outside Buckingham Palace with my MBE and an uncontrollable comb over! It was definitely the most nervous I have ever been but I loved every minute.

2012: On a visit to a winery in Portugal. The cart to my right was still in use and pulled by a beautiful grey mare who was sheltering out of the sun at the time.

2013: Ingliston kindly allowed us to hold a charity talk where I rabbited on to a few people about my life in horses. A great evening and I was very humbled by the amount of people that attended.

In late **2013** I sold up and moved to Aberdeenshire to stay with my son David in the country, just outside Kintore. I simply love it up here. The people have been very welcoming and I have made some great new friends – and there are loads of horsey people too! I miss my friends and family in Ayrshire but I prefer to look at it like I have just expanded my network.

2013: As you can see, the views we get in the morning are not too bad either. Aberdeenshire has some of the most beautiful countryside Scotland has to offer. From Royal Deeside to Dunotter Castle, the scenery is breathtaking. This was taken by my son David just outside our house.

2014: I returned to Berlin to visit the area where I was stationed in 1947. Incredibly the outdoor arena at Glockenturm was still there. The bank jump I am sitting on used to be a tin shed covered in grass. Fortunately it is concrete now but it is in exactly the same place.

2014: The outdoor arena at Glockenturm, Berlin. In the background on the left is the very stadium; albeit expanded now, you see behind me in the earlier picture of Pat and I winning the Allied Forces Championship, 67 years ago!

2014: Sitting in the sunshine at Glockenturm. I sat here on my own for about 15 minutes, just thinking and reflecting. It was a very emotional moment. In many ways it had not changed much. I wish I could have said the same about me!

2014: Taking it easy in my back garden in Aberdeenshire during a photo shoot for my website with my two most prized awards.

2014: The British Touring Car Championship is one of my favourite sports to watch these days. I love it! I was lucky enough to be invited to Knockhill, Fife by 2012 & 2015 Champion Gordon Shedden. If ever you want to see how to compete in sport then look no further than 'Flash'. Gentleman off the track, ferocious on it.

2014: Teaching down in Ayrshire at Ricky Pearson's daughter Clare's yard. It is important for me to get close and explain what I mean when teaching. I am not a fan of shouting across areas. It is impersonal and eye contact is vital when trying to communicate a message. Plus I am deaf as a post these days too! (Photo by kind permission of Erin Walker.)

2014: A fantastic shot of Dykehead Farm in Ayrshire taking from Loudoun Hill for me by local photographer Billy Gibson. Dykehead was my yard for 18 years and I spent many happy years there. The paddock we saw Ramble On and Quando jumping in earlier was just up past the trees on the right of this picture.

2014: Having a little liquid refreshment at Blair Horse Trials near Pitlochry with one of my dearest friends Ann Hamilton. Ann is a great advocate of flat work and a very good teacher too. She has been there through thick and thin and like most really good friends we have a relationship that allows us to let each other know when we're talking nonsense.

2014: One of the bonuses in teaching is when students become good friends. Abbie Ryce is like a granddaughter to me and is one of my biggest champions on Facebook. She and her whole family has been so kind and supportive and I am very grateful. This is us at her family's yard in Cuper, Fife.

2015: Buffalo Bill has always fascinated me as a horseman and showman. Not many people know that he actually toured Scotland with his traveling show. I was lucky enough to visit his museum and grave in the beautiful state of Colorado.

2015: I have been a fan of Western movies all my life and it has always been a dream of mine to visit The Alamo. An amazing experience that I will never forget.

2015: Standing on the corner of Lafayette. One of my favourite photos, taken by my son David. In New Orleans with one of the nicest guys I have ever had the privilege to meet, and a great family friend, David Andrew.

2015: My son David and I in Houston, Texas. David is the engine room behind everything I do these days. An intelligent, generous, good man with a heart of gold. Very proud to call him my son and my friend.

2015: Down in the Yorkshire Dales at Wynbury Stables near West Witton. The Dales is one of my favourite places to visit and I have never had a better teaching experience than working at Wynbury. Nicole Jones and Jill Karadzic are just fantastic and make me feel so welcome every time I visit.

2015: Wynbury used to be Ferdy Murphy's racing yard before Nicole and Jill took it on. The gallops are still very much in use and fantastically set. I was tempted, I can assure you.

2015: Working with Nicole and her German stallion Thor at Wynbury. Note how tidy Thor's front legs are during the jump. This is a great example of one of the traits you should look for when choosing a horse.

2015: Forty years on from my Foxhunter triumph, the Horse & Hound Magazine and Grandstand Media kindly asked me back to the Horse of the Year Show to help the lovely Alice Collins, to my left in red, present the trophy to the 2015 winner. It was a great honour for me and I enjoyed every moment. On the night we had very worthy winners in Rob Maguire and his horse Anastasia Van De Helle. Thanks also to the 23,000 people on my Facebook page that lobbied for this to happen! Really grateful to you all.
(Photo by kind permission of E.S Photography.)

2015: Me and my dogs out in the fields at home in Kintore, Aberdeenshire. These guys give me so much fun. The scamp on the left is Jax and the troublemaker next to me is Corry. Never a dull moment with these boys!

2016: Thurso, Caithness is about as far north as you can go in the UK mainland … and they are horse daft up there! These are the girls from NHC who invited me there to run a weekend seminar. It was great fun and they were so enthusiastic and keen to learn. A brilliant bunch!

2016: Out doing a photo shoot for EQY magazine at Fiona and Morgan Quinell's equestrian centre, The Cabin, near Inverurie, Aberdeenshire. They have been so welcoming to me since I moved to Aberdeenshire and they fly the flag tirelessly for North East of Scotland showjumping. We are lucky to have them up here.
(Photo by kind permission of Angus Blackburn.)

2016: Visiting the stables at Drumtochty, Auchenblae, Aberdeenshire where my father was stud groom over 100 years ago. It was quite an emotional visit and my overarching memory is how peaceful it was. The stables are now wedding accommodation for guests celebrating at Drumtochty Castle but I felt his spirit there for sure.

2016: Holidaying in The Dordogne, France I came across these fantastic sculptures. The artist had made them from pieces of scrap metal and I loved the way he had captured the movement and the essence of the horses.

2016: I love this picture as it encapsulates the spirit of these two so well. Jack and Isabel Mcgeoch are not only both fantastic equestrians, they are great people. They were part of the 'young team' taking over from the likes of myself in Scottish showjumping and they always did it with class and style.

2016: The inimitable Geoff Billington. I have had the privilege of watching him grow from a young boy starting out to becoming a double Olympian. Geoff's jovial and witty personality has entertained us for years. However, it is his horsemanship that makes me smile most. A genius rider who loves horses and competing. Geoff, I salute you too.

My talented daughter Diane painted this for me from a photo my son David shot when he took me away for Christmas to Glencoe, Lochaber after Marjory died on the 10th November 2009. I was torn up inside and felt like my world was over. But Diane and David were there for me all the way and they helped give me the strength to move forward. You never get over losing a loved one but if you have good people around you they help you deal with it. I love them both very much and this picture reminds me why. It hangs pride of place in my kitchen.

it is a two-phase class you will go straight on to your jump off. Make sure you know exactly where you are going after your first phase of jumps and also be aware that your focus will change. A well-thought-out transition from one phase to another could make all the difference in a tight class. Getting the right course information into your head is key so give this part of your preparation the respect it deserves.

Find Your 'Switch'

As the time approaches to compete, you need to be able to sharpen your focus and get into competition mode. For me, it is all about shutting out what is not important at this time, which is everything that does not directly relate to your successful completion of the course. Once this switch is flicked you need to stay 'in the zone'. All you should be focused on now is your round. Forget who has gone clear, those who have not, who is still to come and who is watching… it does not matter. You cannot affect any of that. You can only affect what you are about to do and your focus should only be on that.

It is at this time you check all the tweaks and improvements you have worked on in training and in schooling. You are also focusing on your bond, really getting in tune with your horse. Pop your horse over a few fences in the practise ring, but not too many. It is about getting used to the height you will be jumping at and loosening up. It is not about training and schooling; you have done that part at home. You really just want to get ready for action.

You know at what stage your horse jumps best at home. This is the zone you want to head to. Does it like a good warm up? Does it come out of the traps quickly? Does it tire quickly and lose interest? You also want to involve your support team at this point. Whether it is your parents, your friends or your groom, make sure that when you switch on they know exactly what role you want them to fulfil.

They are there to support you but they cannot do this unless they know what you want.

I always liked to have the team watching what was going on and making sure I was at the ring in plenty of time. At this point I was so focused that I just needed them to be around me and to help make sure I did not break my concentration. Good people around you are essential but it is not good enough that they are just there. They have to be accountable too. They have to perform well. If you have a person supporting you whom you have to constantly push to do the right thing, then they are not supporting. They are hindering and to be brutally honest, they have to go. Your support team has to make the sum of the parts greater than the individual parts. If not, you are not maximising your potential.

Minutes before the competition, what should you have in your head? At a normal show you will be in the collecting ring, you will see your competitors in that ring and although you should be focused on the job in hand you will see things that they do. You can learn a lot by watching where they go wrong. Evaluate what they do, perhaps thinking, 'I would not take that corner like that' etc. When it comes to your time you want to walk or canter your horse in, and feel comfortable riding in a circle outside the starting beam.

When the official blows the whistle or rings the buzzer or bell then off you go. This is what you have worked so hard to do. This is when you begin the course not only physically but also mentally, visualising the round. And one thing to remember finally is pay particular attention to where the finish is. If you jump the last fence and you turn too quick, you can actually miss the beam and be eliminated. I have witnessed this happen so often at shows, so do not get caught out.

Jump To Win

When you finally get into the ring, it is all about controlling your emotions. And the best way to do this, I believe, is by focusing on the course. When it all comes down to it, the course is your path to success with a number of natural highs waiting for you. People sometimes say that the fences and the course are the obstacles you face on the way to winning, but I think 'obstacles' is a negative word. When we started out showjumping as kids did we see fences as obstacles? I know I did not. I saw them as challenges, as the equipment required to stimulate the excitement I wanted from jumping. To enable me to 'Keep Going Clear!'

Clearing a fence well should be one of the most exhilarating experiences we feel. I absolutely loved jumping fences, big and small. That moment when you and your horse are in your bond, almost floating, defying gravity as you sail over the fence without even touching it, that is a feeling to savour and one that put a smile on my face every time. And now you are in the ring you have maybe ten to thirteen of these 'rushes' right in front of you. How lucky are you? This is simply positive thinking. You are now remembering all the good reasons that brought you here.

At this point, you are physically and mentally ready to go. Emotion has had to take a back seat. You can cry, scream or laugh when you win. But right now, you have a job to do. Now, I am not saying that you can simply switch emotion off. It is not that easy and as I spoke about earlier in this chapter, you want to feel the rush that jumping gives you. But it has to be controlled. If you watch the top riders, they are all controlled when they are in the ring. At the level they are competing, in order to win, it is not an option, it is a must! And this cannot be an option for you either.

Winning

The road to ruin is when you ask the horse to do more than you think you can do. Asking too much of your horse and yourself is when the serious problems start. So part of winning is not getting overconfident. Have some belief but never think it is too easy because it is not and never is.

When I won the Foxhunter I achieved something I always wanted to do but I never realised the success it was going to give me. Winning major competitions adds your name to the history books and also shows that you know how to school and train horses. It takes you from holding your father's Irish dray coal horse by the rope to riding royal horses and making history. But winning starts with being humble enough to take criticism and also knowing your limits before you start to work hard and sensibly to exceed them.

Criticism to The Head, Praise to The Heart

As I have already mentioned a few times, always listen to advice. Good advice or bad advice can be stored and remembered later. Criticism is useful, since it shows another person's perspective on your riding, jumping, techniques or even your bond with your horse. Drive and ambition are very important components of success but be sure not to let that drive become stubbornness, meaning that you begin to turn a deaf ear to the evaluation that other people make of you. I always let criticism go to my head and the praise go to my heart. Getting compliments throughout my career from people I respected and admired meant a lot to me but so did criticism from the same people. Their criticism was really guidance and you can learn more from intelligent criticism than sycophantic praise. So put aside the ego and listen humbly to comments so that you can improve. Do not take it personally. There is no better feeling than stretching yourself to achieve something that you previously could not. Comments, criticism and advice you receive can provide valuable lessons that will help you turn failure into success. Life is all ups and downs but you should link them together and attach them to your continual development as a showjumper.

Manage Your Brand

As you achieve success in jumping, the arenas might get more prestigious and the crowds bigger but it is important that your head does not. Stay focused, serious, dedicated and humble. If you look at how the great showjumpers or in fact most sportspeople conduct themselves, they are always professional and respect the sport, the process of training and other competitors. They have trained so hard to get where they are that they understand that a fall or injury could jeopardise all that they have achieved, and so they also work hard to maintain their reputation. This means dealing fairly with everyone and whilst you might get frustrated with your own performance, be sure to keep that to yourself. In fact, get out of the way of yourself and your showjumping ability, by which I mean, do not self-sabotage.

You can criticise your own performance and take issue with yourself but any commentary on others should be accurate but gracious. The comments you make nowadays live forever on social media and in video clips. And always be courteous to stewards, officials and importantly, young riders. Do this and you will soon build a good reputation that becomes your brand. Remember, showjumping is difficult enough without making it more difficult for yourself.

The next chapter looks in more detail at the hardest parts of showjumping: reflecting on your own performance and analysing your faults to improve.

6
Reflection And Analysis

Key Points

What Happened? — Get Back To The Drawing Board — Use Technology — You Cannot Improve On Your Own — To Seriously Improve, Improve Seriously — Apply Improvements To Your Vision

One of the areas that I believe is under-utilised by a lot of showjumpers is the analysing, evaluating and adapting of lessons we have learned from schooling and competition. In this chapter we will focus on how to ensure that we develop a robust system of learning from our day-to-day showjumping journey.

What Happened?
Each show and competition should consist of targets and goals for your jumping, and chances to show what you and your horse can do. View each jump in a competition as an opportunity to demonstrate your skill and your horse's talent and schooling. However,

sometimes things inevitably go wrong and the smart thing to do is to dust yourself down and analyse what happened with a view to fixing it for the next show. Other people are invaluable at this point for giving you their viewpoint on what happened. It is also useful to have one of your friends or competitors film your round so you can see your jumps for yourself as well as how you covered the ground. Once you have identified what happened, then you need to identify why and remedy the cause.

Get Back To The Drawing Board

If you have been taking notes on your training and schooling then you will be able to identify which part of it needs to be focused on to solve any issues. Look over the flatwork and jumping exercises I recommend in earlier chapters and also in the appendix, and start again. As I said at the beginning of this book, the basics are core. For many riders the fault lies in the communication between rider and horse. So scrutinise everything you do. If you still cannot find the cause, then set up the jump or course that gave you the problem and try it again at a lower height, then, all being well, raise it. Remember that your horse may have been affected by the fault so be sure to work on your bond too, making sure the horse's confidence returns and that they start to feel comfortable again.

Use Technology

This is where technology is invaluable. Set up your phone or iPad at various points (with flash turned off) to monitor your progress. Since you never train alone, someone may be able to film it for you. Then watch it back and try to isolate the cause of the fault. Questions to ask yourself might be: Did I do anything to make the front legs/back legs clip the jump? Did we go off on the right legs? Was the horse balanced? Is it the turn or the strides? Think about your hands, your leg position, your feet, your balance and your confidence. Think again too about tack and equipment such as your horse's shoes. Good jumping is about getting all these things right when you put them all together.

You Cannot Improve On Your Own

Consider getting professional advice on your jumping, especially an individual lesson. Although it does cost, it often saves in the long run on a lot of time and energy because it can quickly identify an issue with your riding or your horse that can be sorted out there and then. As with any sport, this tuition can speed up your progress and save you months of trial and error. It also lets you be free to move onto the next stage or next learning point. The risk if you get stuck on one issue is that your interest and confidence start to erode. Keeping an open mind will ensure that you maintain that good fresh attitude. Keep watching, keep learning, keep taking advice and trying new things and you will improve.

To Seriously Improve, Improve Seriously.

I always took jumping and horses seriously and as I discussed in my biographical section at the start, I was taught by some world class instructors and had the privilege to ride some of the best horses in the world. I always wanted to improve and to develop the horses I rode and this was at the core of everything I sought to do. I set myself targets and goals and, if something needed working on, I tackled it head on. When it came to competitions, I knew I needed to be able to concentrate on the course and I could do that by knowing I had done everything I could by way of preparation and training. That way I could achieve the goals I had set myself.

I always wanted to win the Foxhunter and when I did, it was one of the most amazing feelings. But had I not taken every part of training, schooling, horse sense and my own fitness and readiness seriously, then I am not sure I would have managed this. When it

1   0.0200   622.50   12.45

VAT SUMMARY							
CODE	RATE%	GOODS		VAT	GOODS TOTAL	0.040	NETT	25.98
0	ZERO	25.98		0.00			VAT	0.00

TOTAL (GBP)   25.98

REID and ROBERTSON

A Division of Carrs Billington Agriculture (Sales) Ltd

Carrs Billington Agriculture
Montgomery Way
Rosehill Ind Estate
Carlisle
Cumbria
CA1 2UY
Tel : 01228 520212
Fax : 01228 512572
Vat Reg : GB 514 4877 36

Branch Tel No : 01389 752800

OFFICE COPY

INVOICE 101591386
Invoice date : 28-APR-17

INVOICE TO : 87334
Cash Sales Ballagan
Stirling Road
BALLOCH
G83 8LY

GOODS TO : 87334
Cash Sales Ballagan
Stirling Road
BALLOCH
G83 8LY

Tel: 01389 752800

Order No.   : 4738410 28-APR-17 Your ref :
Despatched : 28-APR-17 from Reid & Robertson Ballagan (COLLECTED)
Sales Rep. : 00416 R&R House Account

CODE	DESCRIPTION	PACKS	QUANTITY	PRICE	TOTAL
0720023	Dengie Alfa - Beet (UNMOLLASSED) 20Kg	1	0.0200	676.50	13.53

all comes down to it, so much of my success relied on the level of commitment I gave. It gets back to the questions I asked you in Chapter One: Why do you want to be a showjumper and what does showjumping success look like to you? Visualising and understanding these will help you shape your commitment. Improvement primarily comes from the level of effort and self-evaluation you apply and when you crack this, the rosettes and awards will start to come.

Apply Improvements To Your Vision

As you improve and move through the classes in a show, remember to update your vision of success. First of all, you might want to enter novice, then you might want to win trials and then progress to regional shows. As you and your horse develop together aim to consolidate what you have done by consistently going over the basics but also by expanding what you can do. It is not just about height and speed but about balance, expertise, wisdom and, as I learned all those years ago as a young lad in Berlin, becoming one with your horse. It is also about tricks and tics that improve performance and horsemanship overall. Watch how those who compete internationally work with their horse and you might see small adjustments with their feet or hands. Try some out for yourself and as you think about your goals, envision these improvements being part of your repertoire. The more experienced you are, the more versatile you become and seeing your expanding experience as a component of your progress is key to visualising your success. The next and final chapter wraps up with the essential values and the key messages that I hope you will take from my book.

7
Summary

Key Points

Love Your Horse — Keep An Open Mind — Be Physically Fit — Get The Right Horse — Training & Schooling — Competing — Tack & Equipment — Reflect And Learn — Bond — Be A Student Of The Sport — Be A Winner In & Out Of The Ring

If you have been thinking whilst reading this book that all my suggestions are easy or common sense then I have achieved my aim. When it comes to developing as a showjumper, most things are about preparation and common sense. Indeed, most things in life benefit from applying these values, I have found.

However, the devil is always in the detail and it is wrong to just think that knowing what to do is enough. You have to be able to apply what you have learned and sustain the improvements. In short, make good habits a habit.

So let us recap the content and the key messages.

Love Your Horse

Above all, the safety, respect and care of your horse is paramount. If you do not have this at the heart of your showjumping then, in my opinion, you should quit. It is not fair on you, your horse, your family and friends and your support network. Success in showjumping is not about winning all the time. Success is living the showjumping life in the way it should be lived. Which is working hard, caring for your horse, developing your abilities together, setting a good example to others, committing to improvement and competing fiercely, but fairly.

Keep An Open Mind

I would back the right attitude over ability every time. Sure, you will win a few classes with talent alone but if you really want to leave your mark on the sport then having the right attitude is essential. Having an open mind that constantly wants to learn is a clear advantage. It is so important to make sure that you are a sponge when it comes to showjumping. As I have said, take what you like, leave what you do not like but be open-minded. The human mind is the most powerful computer ever known. If you are not filling it with information on how to be a better showjumper then you are missing a trick. And importantly, you are falling behind the people who are prepared to do this.

Be Physically Fit

Showjumping is not just about how we manage ourselves in the ring. Far from it. It is about a number of component parts culminating in a brief performance that ultimately determines how good we are. We have seen physical fitness evolve in a number of sports over the last 10 to 15 years. Sports that used to be seen as being all about skill and ability have now embraced physical fitness and nutrition as an essential part of the plan. I firmly believe that to improve your showjumping you need to be fit. And the fitter you are, the better you will become. Only those of us who have jumped in a competition know just how strenuous it is to compete. The adrenalin is pumping. Your mind is making hundreds of physical adjustments every second. You are constantly computing thousands of your own thoughts and images whilst guiding, anticipating and correcting your horse's actions. It is a seriously intense workout. This fitness will also protect you too. Showjumping is a seriously tough sport and falling off hurts. I have broken too many bones to list and I dread to think what I would have broken if I was not fit. Fitness helps you take a fall, it helps you heal and it helps you get back on the horse, literally and metaphorically. So please, if you want to be better than you currently are, get fitter.

Get The Right Horse

The right horse will improve your showjumping greatly. Again, this sounds like a given but it is not. So many people end up riding and competing on a horse that does not suit them. If you are serious about becoming a better showjumper then I cannot emphasise enough how important it is to secure a partner that will help you develop. If you are a novice, get a trusted adviser with good experience and work with them as a team. Do your homework before you start looking at horses and base your decision on fact without emotion. Take your time and put the effort in. Be honest with yourself and push hard for value when it comes to buying your new horse.

If you are more of an intermediate rider then apply the same logic but also factor in your experience and where you want to go next. If you are an experienced rider looking to get to a higher level then much of the above is still applicable but it is even more important that you secure an outstandingly talented horse. A great rider can make a good horse better. But I would argue that most riders can only get them so far. Great horses are a rare commodity so due diligence is unbelievably important when you are looking to buy a horse that will compete at national or international level. Put the hard yards in here. A wrong decision can be very costly. The right decision will pay you back in spades.

Training And Schooling

This is where you roll your sleeves up. There is absolutely no way around it when it comes to training and schooling, and neither there should be. You will get out what you put in here, and many times you will actually be short-changed. But you have to keep going and be assured, if you do not train or school enough, you will be found out in competition. And it is not just about practice. It is about good practice. If you keep practising bad habits then you will just become good at bad things. Make sure that you spend time preparing your training plan. Get a good coach that you feel comfortable with. Listen to them. Practise what you are not good at. Practise areas of concern. Practise specifically for an event. Practise the boring bits you do not like doing. Practise for fun. But practise, practise, practise. The more you do something, the better you get. It makes sense. But what you do need to be told is that you are the biggest blocker to your own success. You will look for excuses; it is human nature: "It is too wet." "I am not feeling up for it." "I am too tired." "My horse is not fit." Excuses come in boxes of millions. However, if you want to be a better showjumper, you need to bin the excuses, because trust me, there are others that you will be competing against who are practising like demons and leaving as little as possible to chance. And remember, always use reflection and lessons learned. These are brilliant aids. Feed them back into your sessions and watch how quickly you then develop. I have learned many lessons but I still remember the first lesson I was ever taught: to be humble.

Seek advice from someone who knows rather than someone

who thinks they know. I have heard people who knew nothing give advice and the next thing, the rider was travelling through the air with the horse heading in the opposite direction. Always listen to good advice and do not be afraid to ask.

When I went to shows I watched everything and absorbed all the goings-on around me, and you should too. Also, make a conscious effort to understand how horses think. Get them on your side. I keep banging on about it but when you are both in the ring, your horse is your partner so know and look after your partner and they will look after you.

Competing

To be a better competition showjumper you need to compete to win. Too many people turn up just to take part or they are lacking in confidence, or both. Do not get me wrong, entering a competition for fun is fine if you want to just take your horse out for a wee jump and then go home. But again, you have bought this book because you want tips on how to be better. You want to know how you can compete to win. Of course, all the parts need to be applied and the better prepared you are, the more chance you have of winning. But remember, when it comes to competition, you have to be single-minded. You have to believe that you will win and you have to have a desire to win. You cannot have any sympathy for anyone else during the competition. That does not mean you are arrogant or nasty. You are just focused on competing to the best of your and your horse's ability. Let the chips fall from there.

Before and after the competition, be humble and supportive. That is fine. But when it is time to warm-up and get ready for your class, nothing else matters. Focus is key. You have planned the course with purpose and you know what needs to be done. If you can learn to use this kind of thought process at shows you will become a very dangerous opponent and a serious contender.

Tack and Equipment

Tack and equipment are aids. Yes, they will help, and it is important, vitally important, that you tack your horse in a manner that suits the partnership. However, tack will not make you a better showjumper. Nor will it take away faults in you or your horse. As I outlined earlier, the type of tack you use is dependent on a number of factors and in many ways it is a subjective assessment based on your own preferences and the knowledge you have of your horse and its strengths and weaknesses. As you will have gathered, I am a firm believer in having the minimum amount of mechanics in your horse's mouth. If you need to over-bridle a horse, then more often than not you are papering over cracks. The hard work needs to be done at home. Everything you do at home is a rehearsal for the big stage and there is no greater area to work on than the relationship between your hands and your horse's mouth. Simply fitting a bridle that would stop a train, never mind a horse is not the answer to the problem. The answer lies in working with your horse and making sure that the key areas of control function well and you and your horse understand exactly what is going on and what is expected. And remember, heavy hands do not make a light mouth. Clever hands make a light mouth.

As for the saddle, like your horse, make sure it is custom fitted. Saddle fitters are fantastic and a good one is invaluable. I wish I had had them back in my day! I see a number of people who have poorly fitted saddles and this has a serious impact on how well they go. Do not underestimate this. It can also lead to you and your horse getting injured. So get a proper fitting. As for clothing and accessories, the first thing for me is safety, and the equipment we have now has come on leaps and bounds since I competed. It sends a shiver down my spine when I recall that we used to not even wear a hat when I started. Nowadays we have some fantastic equipment that can quite literally mean the difference between being seriously hurt or just having your pride hurt. Do not worry about your pride. It will heal fine every time. So get equipped.

Take advantage of all the injuries in the past that have been the catalysts for improved safety gear. If you do not, then in my opinion you are nothing short of crazy. And finally, wear the clothing that suits you. Be flamboyant if you want. If it is tasteful, within the rules, and you feel comfortable wearing it, go for it. The more colour and individuality we have in showjumping, the better. Every sport is competing against the others for the next generation of athletes and competitors. If we stay rooted in the past, we will become the past. We need to be respectful of tradition but also open to change and evolution. So if you want to wear a jacket with flowers on it or a fluorescent green hat, as long as you do it with integrity and within the rules, I am all for it.

Reflect and Learn

Without doubt, this in my experience, is the most neglected part of people's showjumping development. Too often showjumpers want to practise practically. In other words, they want to ride their horse all the time. I can understand this because the reason we all do this sport is exactly that, to ride horses. But it is one dimensional and ultimately does not serve you well. I have added a journal section at the end of this book that you can use as an aid to help you log your thoughts on how your schooling, competing, personal issues, competitors, mistakes and successes all impact on your performance and your goals. Reflect. Be objective. Evaluate. Retain the good. Remember the bad. Implement the improvements. Adapting lessons learned will make you a better showjumper but it takes work and commitment. There are no short cuts. If you complete the journal at the back of this book, the information you will gather will astound you and I guarantee you will be able to see things about yourself and your riding that you would have never been able to see previously.

Bond

And finally, there is the bond. Remember the definition of symbiosis? It is the 'interaction between two different organisms living in close physical association, typically to the advantage of both.' This is the 'black arts' part. The bit that I can give no real guidance on other than reiterating its importance and outlining what it means to me. A great relationship between a horse and rider is something that is truly magical. It is a bond, an understanding, a meeting of minds. It is based on trust, respect, discipline, will, and above all, love. And I do not say this lightly. I say it because I am pretty sure that none of us got into showjumping because we liked shovelling dung or enjoyed being thrown to the ground from five feet at 30 m.p.h. via a collection of wooden planks! We got into showjumping because we fell in love with horses. And no matter what you take from this book, always remember this.

To be a good student of the sport I would recommend going to all the shows you can and I would also recommend TV as a way of seeing more showjumping. The showjumping talent now is exceptional and it is advancing so quickly that it is more important than ever to keep up with recent trends, regulations and also technology.

Lastly, to wrap up, I would like to remind you to be a winner in and out of the ring. I hope the tips and advice in this book have helped to develop your understanding of what it takes to be a good showjumper; to compete, to develop your horse to win and most of all, to enjoy it. I often think of Otto Klitski teaching me in the ring back in Berlin and how much a shared love of horses and passion for jumping can add to people's lives. Winning is a wonderful feeling for self-satisfaction but learning about and sharing your life with horses is out of this world. ***Keep Going Clear!***

William Sheret MBE

Development Charts

1) Being A Showjumper

Focus	List reasons & objectives	Goals to achieve objectives
Why do you really want to be a showjumper?		
What does success look like for me as a showjumper?		

If you would like these charts electronically, please email me at willie@keepgoingclear.com

2) Becoming A Better Showjumper

Component parts of becoming a better showjumper	Can I affect these? Yes or no?	By how much? (%)
Natural Talent		
Ability		
Open Mind		
Physical Fitness		
Bond		
The Right Horse		
Training and Schooling		
Competing		
Reflect and Learn		

The above chart is a quick self-assessment and honesty test. Do not think about it too much. Just quickly write down how much you believe you can improve, as a percentage, in each of the above areas based against your current showjumping capability.

Congratulations, if you have put even 1% down then you have identified how you can become a better showjumper and you are on your way to improving. However, I am pretty sure you have put down more than 1% and I am also confident that, if you are honest, you can instantly see a few areas where you can make a significant improvement to your current ability. It is not magic; it is just focus.

3) Checklist For Preparation For Schooling

Areas of Preparation	Date	Evaluation
Are you ready?		
Have you set out what the plan is for the next day?		
Have you got the goals and targets you want to achieve?		
Are the people you need support from briefed and ready?		
Is your horse ready?		
Do you have the equipment required?		
Is your clothing ready?		
Is the tack prepared?		
Is the arena ready?		
Do you know what you want to do with the fences?		

Testimonials

Abbie Ryce: William Sheret MBE or 'Pops' as I like to call him, is the most inspirational person I've ever met! I met him ten years ago and from then it became very clear to me what I wanted to do: I wanted to ride my horses well, learn as much as I could and I wanted to teach others. But having lessons with him made me realise it was not 'teaching' like they do at school. It's about knowledge transfer and passion. That's what helps you become more of a rider, or better! I have taken in so much over the years and I know that it is his guidance, love and passion that has made me, not just the rider, but the person I am today. His style is, honestly, like magic! He just knows how to get the best out of each individual! Not only have I had this with my personal lessons but I have also witnessed it on everyone I have seen him teach! He's just the best! I sure hope I end up half the person he is!

Natalie McAlindon: Was a long time ago now Willie, but I remember how intuitive you were, teaching me to really listen to Shelley and to follow her lead – which meant us working together as a team rather than against each other. You were so gentle in your manner too. Thank you.

Sharon Bruce McKinnon: "Come and jump this fence … it's too small for Jazzie, she needs fences that make her think." Willie would always, after every lesson, make you feel good about yourself and always push you to your limit. He would always know your horses' ability and would always get the best out of me and Jazzie. He left me great memories and achievements with a horse that was my world; now sadly lost but will always cherish. RIP Jazzie and thanks for sharing all your knowledge Willie.

Ella Cummine: Willie taught me and my beloved pony in many lessons, and memories of these lessons are definitely some of my fondest to look back on now that he is no longer with me. Not only does Willie teach with a firm yet considerate approach but he really brought my confidence to new levels and I achieved things in my lessons which I never thought I would, and I am very thankful to him for this.

Rosalind Law: I took a lot from each lesson I had from you. Mainly the confidence to go out and compete again after a 4 year break and I thank you for that!

Johanne Picken: The lesson I had with Willie really helped boost my confidence. I used to be a big scaredy cat when it came to jumping, but he was so calm and supportive. He showed me that there was really nothing to be afraid of. During the lesson, I even managed to jump a fence minus a stirrup and wasn't phased! In fact, Willie even called me a "gutsy rider!" An amazing experience that I will always remember fondly.

Mollie Campbell: My dad bought me my first 'grown-up' horse from Willie after progressing from ponies. Her name was Summer Thursday and gave our family years of happiness. Remember when we came to buy her, you said, "I'll let you ride a great horse', and gave me an amazing lesson. It was a grey you were jumping at the time (mid 70s). Years on I can clearly remember it. You were so kind to a wee horse mad girl.

Ann Hamilton: Willie says to you "Just come and jump the fence again." Miraculously when you come back round it is higher and wider. And miraculously, you clear it.

Maggie Ryce: Willie makes you believe in yourself. We are all better than we think we are and he finds the way to change your thinking and compete. What a boost of confidence he gives you!

Kirsty Boyd: If it wasn't for Willie being as patient as a saint with an 8 year old me not listening to a word he said, then I wouldn't be jumping what I am today. His lessons from an early age gave me such confidence to go on and produce my horses to the height of their ability. The time and effort put in to helping me, both at home and at shows, really means a lot. Thank you!

Allison Bury Fullarton: You taught me as a child and also as an adult after a long break away. You are my inspiration; you bring humour and courage to every lesson and make horses fun – exactly what they should be. Willie, you are truly a gentleman of the horsey world and I wish there were so many more like you. You gave me determination and made me believe I was so much more capable than I thought … can't wait for your book. Love your stories. Love, Ally.

Robert Goldie: When I was a mountie I used to go for a coffee with Willie when he did the Clydesdales. I would tell him about my jumping on a Tuesday night, and the girl I knew with a horse that jumped the first round as fast as the jump off, whether she wanted to or not. Willie's answer was, "Well Bob, that's not show jumping." I never forgot that.

Julie Thwaites: Willie was my showjumping trainer at Camp. Wonderful, calm, kind, knowledgeable teacher. A gentleman and a pleasure to meet him. Such a patient instructor who put up with my numpty jumping!

Mel Morris: I was lucky enough to have Willie as my trainer at an Active Rider training camp weekend. My young horse is good and I've jumped to an OK level in the past, but nerves were getting the better of me due to being out of the saddle for years and on the wrong side of 40! Because of all of this, and bringing on a youngster, I hardly ever pushed myself out of my comfort zone. Willie spotted my horse could jump, kept everything simple, stopped me overthinking and got me riding properly. By the end of day two we were jumping a 1.10+ course with ease. By far the biggest I'd ever done! But it wasn't scary anymore. I believed in him and he believed in us and I always refer back to that lesson when I question myself. Thanks for giving me my much needed mojo!

Clare Wilkinson: Thank you for the brilliant lesson today. Mr Edward had to fairly work today but he enjoyed it as much as I did. Can't wait to get Guinness going with you again.

Emma Daglish: Had a great lesson today off Willie at Wynbury Stables on my new big lump. Thanks, we both enjoyed it a lot.

Annabel Sall: Thank you for my super lesson – a first for me at one metre thirty!

Paige Dryland: After reading a post about William's virtual lesson,

I decided to give it a go and send in my video for a review, and for an extremely good cost as it has helped me on what to improve as I haven't had any sort of lesson in 3 years! His comments were very precise and he picked up on a few things I'd never even thought of, and gave me plenty of things to work on with my horse. After working on these things, I will definitely go ahead with some more virtual lessons. Greatly recommended! Another huge thank you to William for his help.

Lindsay Beresford: Had my first two virtual training session feedback emails from William today! Brilliant feedback; positive and encouraging with lots of good tips and pointers to work on. Extremely good value for money for the level of expertise that William has to offer. Hopefully I can put it all into practice on Sunday at my first BS show in just over 6 months. Can't wait for the next session already! And I will try my hardest to go clear as William says! But most of all relax and enjoy it :) Thanks a lot.

Debby Dunleavy: Thanks Willie. It was great to meet you and thanks for transferring my dressage horse into a show jumper!

Alison Scott: Thank you so much for the great lesson for Megan and Olly yesterday. Baby horse behaved so well.

Linda King: What a day! Brilliant. Willie is a fab guy. Jean is no longer a machine. She has part stag in her now. Everyone had a ball!

Lynn Wylie: Thank you for a super lesson!

Danielle Scott: Had a great lesson today! Cannot wait to try out all the advice you gave me for Bailey. Thank you.

Hollie Rachael Riddell: Just wanted to say thank you for a fantastic lesson today. Really feel that Willow was going much better by the end. I felt loads more confident jumping than I usually do and now I've got plenty to work on! Can't wait for the next one.

Jean Anderson: Thank you so much Willie for training us. It was a pleasure and they were all delighted with how they have done.

Judith Bradford-Knox: A real honour to meet you; a pioneer and a fascinating life. Thank you. Lang may yer lum reek!

Vikki James: Thank you Willie for a super day jumping at Milltown. All the girls enjoyed it and had a huge confidence boost!! Was lovely meeting you and hope to see you again.

Eloise Plant: Loved our lesson today. Look forward to many more!

Helen Pendlowski: Thank you for our lesson at Old Milltimber today. Really enjoyed it!

Andrea Bisset: Thank you Willie for a fabulous lesson. Thoroughly enjoyed it as did Ztar! He is missing his little treats today – he has been looking for you ha ha ha!

Sandra Bogues Ashworth: Thank you so much for a wonderful lesson. Think Macy Grey may be thanking you too. Lol.

Louise Clark: Thanks for a great lesson tonight Willie (and a brilliant chinwag about our favourite animals) My horse and I were completely chilled and relaxed in your company. Your passion shines through in words and actions. Can't wait for next one, and neither can Kiss … she adored you.

Clare Robb: Was wonderful today; seeing an old friend and valued teacher who I first met as a munchkin 5 year old, on a tiny Shetland pony and who has given me many great horse riding lessons and advice throughout the years. Was great reminiscing about old times and made me reflect on the fond memories I have on horses :) Was lovely seeing you Willie or 'Mr Sherbet' as we always said haha! Made me feel really happy today.

Cheryl Wilson: Thank you for a fab lesson on both my horses. Can't wait till the next time.

Emma Logan: Thanks for my lesson today Willie. Loved it! Look forward to getting you back up.

Katie Morrison: Thank you for a fantastic lesson this morning! Horse has never gone so well and I gained such confidence. Looking forward to the next lesson!

Margaret Jones: The lesson went really well. Nice and relaxed and I just jumped the biggest track I have ever jumped. The confidence I took from working with Willie is amazing and what I needed.

Alannah Norquay: Fab lesson today. Loved it! Many thanks Willie!

Rosemary Campbell: What a remarkable man. To hear his story was great and an inspiration to all. He came through life after a humble start and experienced lots of ups and downs and never stopped looking forward. Spoke a lot of sense when it comes to horses.

Georgina Goodwin: Thank you for two great lessons. Your lovely calm manner made me feel confident and reassured. Was really proud of the height my boy ended up jumping (and fillers) Was lovely to meet you.

Pauline Paul: The guru. What springs to mind was when I was warming up in the paddock at Dykehead and you would just see this flat cap coming along the hedges, and your stomach would turn. He was a no-nonsense trainer in his younger days and he pushed you all the time. Simply the best. I love the man.